Rock on Trial

Rock on Trial

Pop music and its role in our lives

Steve Lawhead

Inter-Varsity Press

INTER-VARSITY PRESS
38 De Montfort Street, Leicester, LE1 7GP, England

First edition © 1981 by InterVarsity Christian Fellowship of the United States of America under the title *Rock Reconsidered*.

Revised edition © 1987 by Steve Lawhead under the title *Rock of this Age*.

First British edition © 1989 by Steve Lawhead.

All rights reserved. No part of this publication may be reproduced, stored in a retrieval system, or transmitted, in any form or by an means, electronic, mechanical, photocopying, recording or otherwise, without the prior permission of Inter-Varsity Press.

The lyrics on p. 21 are from 'Money for Nothing', music by Mark Knopfler and Sting, words by Mark Knopfler. © Chariscourt, Ltd. and Virgin Music Publishers Ltd. (PRS). Used by permission of Almo Music Corp. and Virgin Music Inc. All rights reserved. International copyright secured.

British Library Cataloguing in Publication Data
Lawhead, Steve
 Rock on Trial: pop music and its role in our lives.
 1. Pop music. Christian viewpoints
 I. Title
 780'.42

ISBN 0-85110-682-X

Typeset in Great Britain by Emset, London NW10.
Printed in Great Britain by Richard Clay Ltd., Bungay, Suffolk.

Inter-Varsity Press is the book-publishing division of the Universities and Colleges Christian Fellowship (formerly the Inter-Varsity Fellowship), a student movement linking Christian Unions in universities and colleges throughout the United Kingdom and the Republic of Ireland, and a member movement of the International Fellowship of Evangelical Students. For information about local and national activities write to UCCF, 38 De Montfort Street, Leicester LE1 7GP.

To Alice and Ross and to my parents Robert and Lois, for their steadfast support and enduring encouragement.

Contents

Preface   9

1 **Fire is the Devil's only friend**   11
   Rock and the Christian

2 **Stars get in your eyes**   19
   Rock and its image

3. **Starmaker machinery**   31
   Rock and its influence

4. **The heart of rock**   47
   Rock and its beat

5. **Lyrically speaking**   59
   Rock and its message

6. **Every picture tells a story**   69
   Rock and music videos

7. **Too close for comfort**   79
   Rock and the gospel

8. **Give me that old time religion**   89
   Rock and its critics

9. **Sacred cows and Trojan horses**   97
   Rock and evangelism

10. **You gotta have art**   109
   Rock and the standards of art

Preface

It was twenty years ago today...

Well, not quite that long ago, though it seems like it. I wrote this book in 1979 — which is a few thousand years ago in rock 'n' roll reckoning. When it first appeared, there was no Prince, and the King had just recently died; John Lennon was still alive and a Beatles reunion was imminent; no-one had ever heard of Madonna, or Mike and the Mechanics, or Metallica; the second British Invasion was still eating its meals with a spoon; CDs had not been invented, nor ghetto blasters, nor home satellite dishes; music videos were a novelty.

At the time, I considered the book a fair first attempt at joining the debate then raging over popular music in America, a way to inject a little common sense into an often emotional and irrational battle. I certainly never imagined this little soap box of a book (my first) would continue to find an audience into the '90s. But that appears to be the case.

In 1987, the US publisher released a new, updated edition.

There are also German, Swedish and Finnish editions. The entire text has been excerpted in Holland and elsewhere. And now, *voilà!* we have the UK edition.

Consequently, this ancient manuscript has taken on an importance that I never envisaged for it, and I am beginning to feel like the centenarian who complained, 'If I'd known I was going to live so long, I'd have taken better care of myself.' If I had known this book would live so long, I would have written it better. Somehow.

Thus, I feel the need to remind the reader that this is not the last word on the pop world. It was never intended to be. I am a novelist, after all, not a rock critic or sociologist. Nevertheless, it is my hope that this new edition can fulfil its original purpose: to spark discussion, explore a few basic questions, and offer a place to begin thinking seriously about popular music and faith.

chapter 1
Fire is the Devil's only friend

Rock and the Christian

A group of about thirty young people and a handful of adults are standing around a large metal tub, hands in pockets, shuffling their feet. The tub is exactly in the centre of a church car park. The last light of day is fading; and as the shadows stretch across the tarmac, a tingle of excitement grows, a thrill of repressed high spirits.

One by one others are added to the number. Each brings a sacrifice: an armful of flat, cardboard envelopes containing rock 'n' roll records. These are thrown into the tub with the rest. The pyramid-shaped pile continues to grow.

Someone arrives with a guitar and begins to strum a chorus. A few voices join in, and soon most are singing. The night air holds a slight chill now that it is almost dark.

It is time for the ceremony to begin. A leader steps forward, producing a can of lighter fluid which he squeezes liberally over the stack of albums, tapes, books and T-shirts. Now the group falls silent. Expectant.

The man begins to speak, and when he has finished he strikes a match which sputters in the dark, the tiny flare glittering in the reflection of dozens of wide, watching eyes. The group crowds closer around the tub.

The match falls. A flame licks out, climbs the side of the pyramid and races around the inner rim of the tub, igniting the contents. And then, with an audible whoosh! the pyre shimmers in a dancing curtain of fire. The flames illuminate the scene with imperfect animation while, in the tub, objects catch fire, sizzle and melt into one another, coalescing into shapeless masses of cardboard, cloth and plastic. The group joins hands and begins to sing again in thin voices which reverberate across the empty car park. They are singing Luther's hymn 'A mighty fortress is our God.'

So you want to be a rock star

While records burned in that church car park, a few hundred miles north another group was catching fire. This group, an eight-member rock band patterned after the then-popular group Chicago, was performing before an enthusiastic crowd of college students. Called Mother Rush, it was well on its way to becoming an established musical entity in the American Midwest. Big concert dates, recording contracts and thousands of screaming fans figured in the ambitions of the eight musicians.

I shared those dreams of glitter and glory. I was one of Mother's eight children and lead guitar player for the group.

I had played the guitar since I put down my bass clarinet (no future in that) and picked up a secondhand arch-top guitar that belonged to my younger brother. Before long I knew I had to have one for myself. I saved money like a miser and went electric a few months later. I began joining neighbourhood groups in a musical evolutionary process. Natural selection and survival of the fittest guaranteed that the more dedicated or talented members of these neighbourhood groups would stay with the music. The merely curious were weeded out after a while, leaving the serious glory hounds to make the music.

I came up through that evolution. What little native talent I had was considerably augmented by my intense desire to succeed in music. My dedication carried me through five different group incarnations. The only thing any of these groups had in common was the music, the long hours huddled in someone's garage or basement listening to records over and over again trying to capture the sound. Imitation may be the sincerest form of flattery; it is also a short-cut musical education.

Finally, it was college and Mother Rush (the name meant nothing to us, whatever odd images it may conjure up), a group founded on one basic principle: professionalism. Everything about the group was to be professional. I was the only member not majoring in music. We had an accountant who sent us weekly cheques and paid our expenses (a big step up from the usual backstage share out). We tried a novel idea — actually rehearsing an entire show before attempting to line up an audience.

We learned two hours worth of material — album cuts and a few of the latest Top 40 tunes — and then hit the road. The first few times we played were showcase (read: *free*) concerts around the college. Within six months we were the hottest group in the immediate vicinity. In a year's time we were one of the top choices for the college and university circuit in the area and were building a substantial following from forays into surrounding areas as well. Soon there were agents and publicity and talk of record deals. But in the end we decided to quit while we were still ahead. We disbanded amicably on graduation and split the money we had been saving to pay for demo tapes, more sound equipment and a bus.

So Mother Rush faded from the scene. I had delved further into rock than most of my friends, and certainly further than the general population. Like the people I played for, I had grown up on rock music. But I had also grown up in the church. I had become a Christian in high school — somehow never considering anything wrong with being a Christian and a rock musician at the same time.

After the band broke up, I did not think about playing rock 'n' roll seriously anymore. As much as I enjoyed it, that part of my life had reached a natural conclusion and was put aside. I did not become a musician; I became a writer. After attending Northern Baptist Theological Seminary, I joined the staff of the American magazine *Campus Life*.

As an editor for *Campus Life* I created the 'First Impressions' music review column, which put me in touch with the burgeoning Christian music industry. Through the column I was introduced to a couple of Memphis musicians, Ed DeGarmo and Dana Key. My interest in their careers brought an invitation to manage for the DeGarmo and Key Band. Upon leaving my post at the magazine I formed a contemporary Christian record label called *Ariel*. Due to circumstances well beyond my control, *Ariel* 'went lead' (as opposed to 'going gold') after a little more than a year. And it was back to writing.

Through these experiences I've had the opportunity to learn about popular music, how it's made and sold, and the business apparatus behind it. I've also had a chance to organize my thinking about what I had previously accepted on an intuitive level.

The 'First Impressions' column put me right up on the front lines of an active, ongoing war over rock music — a smouldering, sputtering volcano of a war that erupts from time to time in the flames of heated conflict. It's a war I've been involved in one way or another ever since, often as a reluctant crusader who would prefer listening to the music rather than analysing it. But, as they say, I knew the job was dangerous when I took it.

The IN basket

Over the years I have received hundreds of letters regarding various aspects of rock music. Here is a sampling:

> Don't you know that rock music is of the devil? When will God's people learn to leave this worldly junk alone and follow Christ? F. G.

> The evil of rock and roll isn't only in the beat, which is sinful, it's also in the lyrics — which incite all kinds of unchristian behaviour. Thinking otherwise is only wishful thinking — not reality. S. B.

> You only have to listen to one song on the Top 40 to

ROCK ON TRIAL

know that Satan is in the driver's seat where rock music is concerned. G. W.

Other letters expressed genuine confusion:

> I just became a Christian last week and threw all my heavy metal records away because it didn't seem right to listen to them anymore. But now what am I supposed to do? Is there any Christian music for someone like me? D. M.

> I'm always hearing how Christians are supposed to be against popular music because of the beat and words. I for one believe that it's up to the individual to choose — that's what God gave a mind for, wasn't it? C. B.

> What about Christian rock? What about musicians like Sheila Walsh or The Fat Band — their music is just as good as anything you'll hear on the radio, yet the message of God's love comes through loud and clear. What's wrong with that? A. H.

Positive, negative or merely confused, I get their letters, and the controversy does not appear anywhere close to being resolved. Each development on the popular music front raises new issues, new questions, new conflicts. And as contemporary Christian music — what used to be called 'Jesus Rock' — continues to break new ground, gaining wider acceptance and increased visibility in the music marketplace, new issues arise:

☐ Is it wrong for Christians to be associated so closely with images of success and glamour?

☐ Can music be authentically rock and legitimately Christian at the same time?

☐ Can Christian values be transmitted through rock music, or is it intrinsically corrupt?

☐ Does acceptance means compromise?

The issues surrounding rock music and its place in popular culture are as alive as ever and still capable of stirring up deep feelings.

I want my MTV

Anyone in America who cares to catch up on rock's latest exercise in wretched excess has only to tune in to MTV or 'Friday Night Videos' — or any programme featuring music videos (by one estimate, there are now more than 300 such programmes in the States) — and if unprepared, you might think your TV had entered the Twilight Zone. The UK, Australia and other countries are also moving in this direction with all-hours TV and satellite pop channels.

Spliced into the usual stock footage of musicians dressed like glittery refugees, playing their instruments on a stage awash in coloured lights and machine-produced fog, you'll see video montages of pop stars prowling through deserted back streets, growling out their tormented songs. You'll see slinky cars and fast girls, plush apartments, neon to rival the Las Vegas strip or Piccadilly Circus, and enough chains and leather to outfit any dozen motorcycle gangs—all of it served up with enough video gimmickry to flesh out a graphic designer's nightmare.

But rock's excesses are not limited to its new format. You pick up the newspapers to read about a teenage suicide victim whose last moments of life were played out to the accompaniment of an Ozzy Osborne song entitled 'Suicide Solution.' You hear a song on the radio that drifts sinuously by — what's that, something about 'Sugar Walls?' — listen closer and discover a paean to the female genitalia. Or you catch yourself humming a catchy little tune, only to realize it's a none-too-subtle advertisement for the gay lifestyle.

You wonder, 'Is it just my imagination, or are some of the groups actually getting weirder and rougher?' The radio cranks out songs more blatant and suggestive then ever, laying bare the sex act, wondering about the perverse and unnatural. Some musicians denigrate their audiences and openly brag about the money they make by ripping off their fans, treating life like one big party filled with pills and booze.

This book is an attempt to make sense of rock music, to separate the real dangers from the imagined, to lend some helpful perspective to the whole chaotic scene by articulating the problems and proposing solutions, to point the way out of the morass.

▶ chapter 2

Stars get in your eyes

Rock and its image ▶

ROCK ON TRIAL

You are sitting in a jam-packed, smoke-filled concert hall. Slowly the house lights dim, a hush falls over the crowd, and a voice booms out from nowhere, 'Ladies and Gentlemen, KXSS proudly presents...' Suddenly the darkened stage leaps to life under a flash of white light, and there they are, shimmering in a rhinestone and sequins blaze. The music starts, stirring you, lifting you. It is so wonderful, so glamorous, so thoroughly exciting. You begin to think a life of spotlights, fancy clothes and appearances before thousands of adoring fans would be just about perfect.

▶ *Problem: Rock music is presented and promoted in a highly attractive manner. The glitter and glamour conceal rock's true antihuman nature.*

As a musician, I travelled with Mother Rush hundreds of miles every week. We would meet Thursday or Friday afternoon to load our equipment into a rented trailer. Then we would pack our bags and pile into the van and head out on the highway. The next sixty hours would be nonstop — nonstop travel, nonstop togetherness, nonstop monotony, nonstop boredom — until we rolled in again at five o'clock Sunday morning.

After a while all the motels and cheap café diners and

petrol stations look the same. (You've heard this before; eventually most songwriters commit it to song.) The road wears on you. The empty hours wear on you. Typically, a musician spends twenty-two hours a day waiting for two hours of life in the spotlight. And the waiting is deadening.

But part of the illusion of show business is that the glitter of the bright lights touches every area of the performer's life. This illusion is as far removed from reality as chalk is from cheese. The spotlight hides more than it reveals. The life of a performer is difficult, sometimes intolerable and often dull. Yet in the Mother Rush days, we never wanted for enthusiastic friends and followers to tag along with us on band trips. There were often so many people crammed into the van that we dubbed it the Rolling Armpit. Enough said.

The glare of the spotlight holds great attraction — especially for young people, and anyone else easily impressed with a little flash and dash. For those unacquainted with the stark reality of the road, the illusion of glamour and prestige is synonymous with the music, and one is idolized as much as the other. The latest and maybe best attempt on the part of a rock group to present *their* side of the story comes from the British band, Dire Straits, who satirized the performing life to wonderful effect in their send-up 'Money for Nothing.' In it, an ignorant, lazy, jealous appliance-store shop hand sits glued to the MTV non-stop pop channel and laments:

> I should'a learned to play the guitar,
> I should'a learned to play them drums...
>
> Look at them yo-yos, that's the way you do it!
> You play the guitar on the MTV
> Oh, that ain't workin' — that's the way you do it!
>
> You get yer money for nothing,
> Get yer chicks for free.

Most performers are content to create and maintain their version of the illusion, cutting out larger-than-life figures for themselves to sell to the public; it's hardly surprising that fans covet the illusion.

Mick Jagger and the Rolling Stones adopt an air of arrogance and decadence. ZZ Top, rock 'n' roll's good ol' boys, grow beards and launch the 'Howard Hughes of Blues' tour. Boy George creates a stir with his outrageously androgynous appearance, while Prince and Madonna mince their way to the top of the charts with steamy stares and baldly suggestive videos. Bruce 'The Boss' Springsteen puts on a jeans jacket and becomes the working man's hero.

These are all poses, images — a necessary part of show business. We *want* our entertainers and stars to be the biggest and the best, or at least different from us in some obvious way. We *want* the vicarious thrill we get seeing Somebody. An ordinary nobody does not rate a second look. It is no wonder performers put on a glittery front.

Sadly, the illusion is perpetuated and indulged — by performer and fan alike — to the point that we can no longer distinguish fact from fantasy, image from art. What is meant to enhance reality replaces it. Performers begin to think of themselves as the characters they play. The audience believes that what it sees on stage is real.

Rock musicians work hard to create an image (all-American boy, rebel, darling, pervert or weirdo) and constantly reinforce this image with their actions. Most performers are happy with the arrangement, since their public life bears little resemblance to their private life. Thus the artfully contrived image protects their privacy. In public they can slip into their stage persona, thereby leaving their private lives safe. The greater the distance between real life and their stage personality, the more secure their privacy.

Rebels with, or without, a cause

How did these rock illusions take shape? In the early days of rock 'n' roll the musicians were cast as rebels. Rock was called the music of rebellion, though in real life the musicians were not rebelling much against anything.

The rebel image of early rock 'n' roll got a lot of publicity in the popular press. The music *was* different. Bill Haley and the Comets stumbled onto a hybrid blend of country-western, swing and rhythm 'n' blues that had a special appeal. Their recording of 'Rock Around the Clock' in 1955 became the first rock 'n' roll record to achieve number one national status, bringing this new kind of music to national attention. (The phrase 'rock 'n' roll' had been introduced in 1951 by American DJ Alan Freed on his radio show, and several black artists had already flirted with the form, but as yet it had not caught on.) 'Rock Around the Clock' made Bill Haley rock's first superstar. Fans rallied to him, a slightly chubby, benign uncle-figure in bow tie and Brylcream, quite unused to the commotion he caused wherever he went.

The wild enthusiasm of Haley and his music kicked off the rebellion image in music. The underdog's struggle against oppressive authority had become a popular literary theme and was being reinforced in films such as *Rebel without a Cause* and *Blackboard Jungle*. The latter film used the song 'Rock Around the Clock' under its opening credits. Released two years previous, and only mildly successful, the song's inclusion in the film created an instant sensation.

Blackboard Jungle — about a teacher (played by Glen Ford), who struggles to impart some basic values to a group of hardened, street-wise kids only to be rebuffed — was released to pandemonium. Fans loved it; critics and authorities hated it. Russia denounced it as a capitalistic plot to subvert their children. In Britain mobs rioted in the streets. Elsewhere it was publicly condemned and the film confiscated by various local authorities. For this and other reasons, rock music was quickly branded as outlaw music — an image which has sometimes increased its popularity and at other times limited its appeal, but one which it has never managed to shake.

If Bill Haley was not particularly roguish in his baggy pants and plaid sports coat, along came Elvis with his dark, smoky good looks, greased-back hair and dangerously curled lip. Elvis radiated a sex appeal which made Haley look like an old shoe. The fact that adults could not stand Elvis made him all the more desirable as a prime teen commodity. Adult resentment grew into a fierce dislike and, consequently, Elvis's success was assured.

Newspapers and magazines reported Elvis's every sneer. They were warming to the idea of rock stars and rock 'n' roll as a great source of lively, controversial stories. By 1956 rock 'n' roll stories were common, taking one of two forms: 'Let's all have a laugh at the new lunacy,' or 'Rock 'n' roll is taking us to hell in a handbasket.' Still, most people thought that rock 'n' roll was merely an unfortunate fad that would soon go the way of goldfish-swallowing, jitter-bugging and phone-booth stuffing.

But time rolled on and rock had no intention of giving up the backbeat. The media which had forecast its death every year since its beginning took on a new slant. Silly stories — 'look what the crazies are doing now!' — ceased, and outright attacks became common. Decent citizens stood four-square against the 'child corrupters.' It did not matter if rock 'n' roll was rebellious in content or not, a rebellion formed around it. Soon it became an act of defiance just to listen to rock 'n' roll music. The antisocial image grew and so did the tension surrounding it.

This tension is ever present, breaking out in something close to real conflict from time to time. Periodically, artists like Lionel Richie and Ric Astley and groups like Ah Ha and Kylie Minogue come along to launder rock's soiled image and put on a well-scrubbed front. Yet for every Lionel there's a Prince eager to drag the newly polished image through the muck again. Still, all this tension and conflict is focused on the illusion.

An exercise in peeling oranges

Rock musicians are actors. The world of contemporary

culture is their stage. What they say about themselves and their music is like so many lines from a continuing play. Bob Dylan used to tell people that he was a vagabond orphan to hide the fact that he was from a middle class family named Zimmerman.

Boy George shaves his eyebrows, paints his face, dons a geisha girl outfit, and next thing you know everybody's wondering, 'Well, is he a *he* or isn't he?' It's the stuff gossip columns are made of. Performers are creating, enhancing, remaking their images all the time — it's part of the illusion. Not everything they say or do should be taken seriously.

Although the performers may know where the illusion leaves off and reality begins, it's harder for the audience. We are left to struggle with the illusion, which, in absence of all the facts, is all we see. Still, in fighting the illusion and wrestling with the image, real conflict often develops, conflict which can divide families and cause deep wounds. There were sometimes more fireworks in an evening discussing some of my music with my parents than Ozzy Osborne uses in a year — and my parents at least tried to understand!

Sadly, much of the conflict is unnecessary. It can be avoided once we get a handle on some of the main problem areas. To understand rock accurately, we must penetrate the illusion and separate the image (rebellion, violence, glamour or whatever) from the reality (making music).

Consider, for example, professional wrestling, which relies heavily on show-biz tactics to draw spectators. Wrestlers with names like Big Daddy, the Masked Assassin or the Screaming Russian strut before the camera, foaming at the mouth with false bravado and wild promises of mayhem, disgrace, humiliation and defeat for their enemies. 'I'll break that guy's neck, so help me. If I ever get my hands on him, I'll kill him! After what happened in Kansas City (or Birmingham or Perth or wherever), he's dead meat and he knows it. This will be the match of the century...'

ROCK ON TRIAL

If anyone dreamed that these maniacs were serious, none of them would be allowed to walk the streets. But professional wrestling is so transparently phony, the theatrics are so old and clichéd, no-one believes them. If you wanted to talk about the *sport* of professional wrestling, you would quickly discard the petty dramatics. In a sense, that is what I would like to do with music — deflate the illusions and talk about the 'sport,' the music known as rock.

Actually, pro wrestling and rock have more in common than we might first realize. Both are firmly rooted in the entertainment business. Look at the rockers of the sixties or the more recent punk and heavy metal rock scene and you will find the same elements found in pro wrestling — insane bragging and arrogance, absurd posturing, cultivation of outlandish appearances and bizarre behaviour. Even their names have the same corny ring of the melodramatic: Twisted Sister, Motley Crue, Poison, The Dead Kennedys. The only major difference is that professional wrestlers are known for the phonies they are, while rock musicians, unfortunately, tend to be taken more seriously. They should not be.

Think of rock music and all its trappings as a big navel orange. If you want to eat the orange, you must peel away the thick, indigestible rind to get to the fruit. If you tried to eat the orange without peeling it, you would get a very wrong impression of the fruit. The taste and texture would be too confusing to enjoy. It is much the same with rock. For any discussion to have meaning, we must, as much as possible, peel away the images and illusions which confuse the issue, and separate them from the notes-on-paper music. The meat of the fruit is what we want to talk about, not the peeling. Unfortunately, when some people set out to talk rock, they take one bite of the rind and declare the fruit inedible.

In the early days, rock was considered by many to be a most virulent expression of Communist activity aimed at undermining the moral character of the West's youth. While

STARS GET IN YOUR EYES

it's been quite a while since anyone has seriously suggested that the Kremlin calls the tune rock dances to, equally ludicrous ideas abound. Notions like 'backward masking' — the practice of recording a musical bit backwards, ostensibly to influence a listener subliminally — continue to bamboozle the gullible.

This is not to say that performers do not occasionally attempt to use their charisma to influence their fans. A recent example was the monumental Live Aid concert. Organized by artist Bob Geldof of the Boomtown Rats, Live Aid was a daylong, satellite-assisted international rock extravaganza which to date has raised 150 million dollars in relief for famine-stricken Africa, and spawned similar projects around the world such as Sport Aid, Farm Aid and the Nelson Mandella concert (for racial equality in South Africa).

As worthy as these causes may be, whenever entertainers attempt to use their public image to sway popular opinion we should be wary. We need to ask ourselves, 'What does this musician know about_____?' Fill in the blank: nuclear power, saving whales, apartheid, banning the bomb, stopping a war, battling with a famine. Some may know a lot and some may not; some issues are straightforward while others are highly complex.

Of course everyone is allowed to voice his or her ideas. But we must carefully scrutinize any public personality (rock musician, sports hero, television star, film actor) who ascends to the soapbox. A sceptical outlook is a basic requirement for all of us living in the media age.

Since rock musicians are image manipulators, most often what they say and do has a purpose. Usually that purpose is simply attention. They want or need to stand out from the crowd. Some artists will say or do anything to be noticed, the more bizarre and shocking the better. So they dye their hair green, dress like gypsies or space cadets, talk about overthrowing the empire, or advocate free atomic waste allotments for infant school children — whatever will give the most attention at the time. A sceptical person knows these antics to be nothing more than strands of the illusion which are important to the artist because they help obscure the all-too-plain truth that, ultimately, rock stars are just ordinary people. Beneath the eye shadow and spandex tights they are very much like the rest of us.

In order to discuss rock music seriously we must be aware of the illusions and not get caught up in the superficial trappings such as hair, clothes, language and styles of life. Therefore, keeping an open mind (as well as a sceptical outlook) will help us to sort out and debunk much of the nonsense and concentrate our attention on the real issues which, unlike professional wrestling, do exist in rock.

Promoting the pop product

Part of the reason it is so difficult to separate the illusion from reality is because rock music, like many other products of pop culture, regularly promotes its illusions as the product itself. In other words, they aren't selling the steak, they're selling the sizzle.

Rock music is a product — records, tapes, compact disks bought and sold in shiny, alluring covers featuring beautiful people. They are advertised, promoted, pumped up, hyped for all they are worth — and far beyond their worth. There is music mixed in too, but the larger commodity being sold is the experience, the atmosphere, the status that comes with owning the product. And since rock music is the expression of a quickly changing culture, immediacy is a large part of the package.

The issue is not that the attractive package conceals rock's dangerous side but rather that the package has become the product. It is not that unsuspecting people are being sold something they do not want or would not buy if they were told the truth. No, people buy rock because they want what the package offers. They want to participate in the illusion of glamour, excitement and fast living which the promotion promises, and which the music appears to deliver.

Rock music is a chameleon which becomes what its

listeners imagine, taking on the colour of individual fantasies. At this level it becomes nearly impossible to separate the illusion from the art. They are the same thing. Here, too, is where the utmost in open-minded scepticism is called for. Fortunately, most people are naturally sceptical and level-headed enough not to want to emulate all the weirdness going on in the rock and pop world. But some do.

Some, through an unfulfilled need for attention, belonging, esteem or whatever, do seek to copy in their sphere of reality what they see taking place in the rock world. This is the problem.

But it is a problem much larger than rock music itself. It is a social problem that extends to modern culture at large and finds expression not only in music but in such unlikely things as cars, alcohol, sports and fashion, in anything which touches culture and can be packaged and sold as a product.

Rock is seen as more of a threat, however, because it offers shelter for certain antisocial tendencies. Therefore, it draws more concern than, say, the fact that certain grown men buy ultra-expensive, high-performance sports cars to do nothing but drive the mile and a half to work — they don't hurt anybody. But someone who wants to take drugs because his favourite rock star takes drugs *can* get hurt.

chapter 3
Starmaker machinery

Rock and its influence

ROCK ON TRIAL

The average life of a star is about two years; superstars shine a little longer. While riding the crest of popularity, a superstar's influence seems awesome. Whether this influence is illusory or not, the power seems quite real.

Rock musicians often enjoy the same social status as statesmen or royalty. They walk in worlds of larger-than-life dimensions where every move is publicized and reported by the gossip columnists. Fanzines spew out a never-ending stream of syrupy sensationalism and pre-posed photos over the moment's heart-throb.

Occasionally, the public becomes indignant over what it sees transpiring in these golden lives. Rock stars are notorious for stirring up the public wrath in one way or another.

▶ *Problem: The lives of rock musicians are morally corrupt. Since these stars are worshipped by their fans, their immoral actions have a great impact. Basic human values are undermined and their followers are influenced steadily, and sometimes unconsciously, towards immorality.*

A thousand years ago small groups of uncultivated, bizarrely dressed, oddly named musicians travelled from town to town, singing and accompanying themselves on the vielle (a stringed instrument). The most famous of these — Jumping Hare, Little String, Ladies Praiser and Rainbow — were rewarded with such fame and luxury that they were imitated by hordes of less gifted, envious men. During the late Middle Ages chronicles refer to 'large armies of minstrels,' the better ones playing for nobility while lesser troupes entertained at peasant celebrations. Despite the demand for their performances at all levels of society, these itinerant poet-musicians were held in contempt throughout the era. The animosity stemmed principally from the Church, which held that their obvious secular *joie de vivre* posed a threat to the spiritual welfare of its people.[1]

It would seem that we have not changed much in a thousand or so years. Migrating armies of musicians still roam the land — caravans of diesel trucks and converted coaches. The more famous make huge heaps of money and live in unstinting luxury, to be imitated by the less lucky who also strive to make mounds of money and live in luxury. And the whole scheme is held in contempt by the guardians of the collective moral conscience.

Popular music has been seen by some as an eroding agent on humanity's spiritual well-being, a rat in the cellar gnawing at the 'new wine' keg. Popular musicians have sometimes been cast in the role of Pied Piper, leading their all-too-willing followers down the primrose path to sin.

The question of influence is really a knotty problem, bound up as it is with theories of human development, cultural considerations, morality, values and various items of media baggage. The question at the root — 'How is human behaviour influenced?' — opens onto such an untidy landscape of current thought that one is tempted to cruise by the more obvious landmarks and pass the rest without a glance.

While some rock stars merely cultivate an immoral image, others are actually immoral. Do immoral rock artists have a bad influence on their fans? 'Yes, of course,' we say, and move on to something else, such as how much money and fame their displayed immorality brings them.

Walls and windows

The best-accepted views of human development posit that one's parents (or 'significant other,' or 'caregiver') are the single most influential force in a person's life. Further, it is believed that within a few years after birth, each child is endowed with the major portion of his or her personality components and most, if not all, of his or her moral values. Most psychological theorists suggest that we become what we are and what we will be at a very early age — some say as early as five, others indicate later on, somewhere between eleven and fourteen. Whatever the case, the short trouser years are extremely important; we change only slowly and with great difficulty after them.

But people *do* change, for better or worse despite what kind of upbringing they may have had.

Research into personality development shows that people are most vulnerable to influence and, therefore, to change in the areas of their greatest needs. On a physical level we all need food to survive. If we were long without food, we would, regardless of age or IQ, become vulnerable to the influence of anyone who promised to give us food. In the same way we are vulnerable on a psychological level. We all have basic psychological needs: acceptance, self-esteem, affection. If these basic needs are denied or withheld, we become vulnerable to the influence of anyone or anything which promises to fill those needs.

As we get older we look to fulfil our needs more and more apart from our families. Thus, personal friends and peers become more important toward adolescence and so we become more vulnerable to their influence. We look for role models to imitate, trying various possibilities before settling into one which wears comfortably — for the time being.

But, people are not chameleons, forever changing to fit the demands of their surroundings. Eventually, mature human beings emerge which stand on their own, apart from parents or peers. The time for role models passes as the soft, mutable core hardens into a solid personal identity. After that, only for brief intervals is the solidified personality vulnerable to change, depending on outer and inner circumstances or on various developmental stages throughout life.

These opportunities for change might be thought of as windows which open and close periodically throughout life. When the windows are open, the personality is vulnerable to influence. When the windows are closed, the personality actually resists change and may even be somewhat hostile to it — the window becomes a wall, keeping out whatever influences may gather outside.

The windows of vulnerability are open wide during the first months and years of life; they close slowly and remain closed until the beginning of adolescence when they again open wide. The windows close again after adolescence and open a crack only briefly at the beginning of young adulthood. The windows of vulnerability will open several times more before old age. Of course, the windows of vulnerability can be forcibly opened by any number of very strong circumstances brought to bear on the personality.

The most important interval for our discussion is during adolescence when tremendous mental, physical and emotional upheavals begin, and when the larger world outside the family takes on great attraction. This is the time when rock music becomes a magic carpet to an individual fantasy world populated with scores of like-minded, like-bodied, like-spirited comrades.

Culture clubs

There is a large, active and aggressive youth culture in many countries throughout the world. Perhaps in no other time in history has there been so much available to so many at such a young age. Those entering the youth culture are greeted with clothing styles, language, entertainment and rules of behaviour all their own. All young people, with few exceptions, participate in this highly sophisticated, highly complex youth culture.

We live in a pluralistic culture of sheltering and supporting many different roles, modes of behaviour, world views and lifestyles. And in this mix people with nothing in common but their age — never mind upbringing, education or economic status — can join the youth culture club merely because they are young and share the desire to discover life. This is the strength of the youth culture and the very thing which terrifies parents and adults. The window is wide open, and anything can fly in.

While young people may make up the youth culture and participate in it, they do not actually create it. Instead, the various elements of the youth culture are copied or recycled from the larger adult community, or are devised especially for young people by adults, as in the case of clothing, entertainment, cosmetics and other accoutrements. Although the youth culture may willingly embrace these trappings, they tend to be dictated by older tastemasters. Thus, a young person can turn up at a rock concert arena wearing clothes from a favourite boutique, talking like a favourite television star, drinking the beer of a favourite football or cricket player, striking poses from favourite films.

Adults, genuinely alarmed by what they see taking place among the young, look for an explanation for all the negative things they see going on: drinking, promiscuity, drugs, rebellion. 'After all,' some say, 'we didn't teach them to act this way. It must be those rock performers!'

That's a handy explanation. But it calls for a quantum leap in logic that is far from honest. Young people are not exactly powerless pawns of pop culture. By their acceptance or rejection of various elements, they continually transform the culture that surrounds them. What may appear from the outside to be a vast, impenetrable private domain is really a highly transient, unstable sea of change when seen from within. The tributaries which feed this sea are innumerable, or nearly so.

This mix of influences can be seen as a spiral. As young people enter the youth culture, they come under its influence and in turn exert influence on it, changing it only to be further influenced, and so on. Does the spiral ever stop? No, but young people eventually stop responding to the cues of culture; they simply grow out of it. Their windows of vulnerability close, and they assemble an adult personality from the mix of elements they have chosen from the myriad of possibilities.

This is the scary part: what if the things they chose are personally damaging, morally reprehensible or socially unacceptable?

Some say that music, like other forms of art, does not influence culture but simply reflects it. Others say that a powerful, dynamic art form such as rock music goes far beyond merely reflecting its culture to actively influencing it. The truth is, I think, somewhere between the two. Performers know what their audiences want to hear, so they try to deliver the goods (reflection); they also know that to remain popular they have to stay just a half-step ahead (influence). It is a cat-and-mouse game played by intuition.

Many performers merely exploit the current trend to cash in on the sound of the moment. This is crass commercialism. Commercial exploitation's sole aim is to promote an acceptance of its product by misrepresenting its popularity or nature. This is true of other consumer products too, not just music. A soft-drink maker, for example, airs a television commercial that shows *everyone* in an entire village drinking that brand, simultaneously! 'Be part of the gang; don't get left behind!' That is the commercial appeal. Commercialism works similarly in music by distorting the music's importance, making it seem well nigh world-shaking. And since popular music is basically commercial music to begin with, it would seem that its power to influence, to move people to act, is enormous. But it isn't.

Granted, the vulnerable individual may be overwhelmed by a gravitational field too strong to resist and too enticing to avoid. There is the risk that a sensitive personality may crash-land on a harsh and alien world. Stranded. Lost. Prey to a host of modern horrors.

In such a case, it is not enough to be concerned merely with removing the more obviously obnoxious elements of a culture. The problem of creeping immorality in society simply cannot be cured by removing a relative handful of rock renegades. Anyone who suggests that it can is like a one-pill doctor bent on treating a score of maladies with a single stock remedy. Not only is the result ordained to failure, it can jeopardize the life of the patient.

A legend in our own time

The mistake of placing the blame for a generation's perceived demise at the feet of any one particular obnoxious influence can be clearly illustrated by a quick look at the life of that archrenegade-turned-respectable: Elvis.

At his height, Elvis was everywhere at once, and his fans were legion — screaming hordes of teenagers, crying, dying, for a look at him. His concerts were legendary. Tony Palmer recounts, 'He came on leering and twitching, his hair all down his eyes, his grin lopsided. The moment the music started he went beserk. Spasms rocked his body as if it had been plugged into the same electrical source as his guitar. His hips began to grind, his legs vibrated like power drills. He pouted and humped and walked as if he were sneering with his legs.'[2]

Television producers allowed him only to be shown from the waist up. Neither TV presenters nor producers would risk public outrage by showing Elvis undiluted; he was just too strong for family viewing.

From the beginning it seemed that nobody except his fans had any use for Elvis.

Critics loathed him, preachers called him sinful; in Miami, he was charged with obscenity; in San Diego, the city

STARMAKER MACHINERY

fathers voted to ban him altogether — unless he omitted from his act all 'vulgar movement.' A Baptist pastor in Des Moines declared him 'morally insane.' According to the East German Communist paper *Young World*, Elvis Presley was a 'weapon of the psychological war aimed at infecting a part of the population with a new philosophical outlook of inhumanity...to destroy anything that is beautiful, in order to prepare for war.'[3]

How embarrassing! The Communists, who had long been accused of trying to pervert our country's youth as part of their master plot to conquer the world were now levelling the same accusation at us. 'Elvis is corrupting our children!' If he was, the children of the world could not have cared less.

Soon there was Elvis everything: T-shirts to toilet paper, bobby socks (fluorescent, yet) and bubble gum, ball-point pens, lipstick, autograph hound dogs and Bermuda shorts. And films. Elvis starred in a string of smash hits which kept him before his loyal public. And the coins kept rolling in. He amassed a personal fortune amounting to hundreds of millions of dollars.

Years passed and after several artfully contrived comebacks, Elvis remained King of the Rock, eventually reaching the pinnacle of acceptability — performing for the president of the United States. Not only did he appear before President Nixon, he is probably the only performer to receive his customary fee for this command performance. A few more years passed; then, unexpectedly, Elvis was dead at the age of forty-two. Millions mourned his passing. The King was dead. The world wept. And continues to weep, as fans from all over the world trek to Graceland Mansion to lay wreaths on his grave by the swimming pool, or gather to light candles in his memory.

What happened? How did this greasy-haired kid from Tupelo, Mississippi, chief child corrupter and exponent of open rebellion become acceptable, respectable even?

What happened is that we just got used to Elvis. The

ROCK ON TRIAL

young people of the fifties grew up with him, and the older folks, after living with him for a while, decided that he wasn't so bad after all. Very rich and very famous, Elvis became a folk hero.

Elvis did not change so much as our perception of him changed. (In fact, his immorality quotient was demonstrably higher in his later years than in his youth when he so scandalized the world.) He was no longer that obscene young man who was leading the world to ruin. He was the Sun King who owned a Southern mansion where tour buses full of little old ladies stopped. If you were lucky, you could scramble out and snatch a handful of gravel from his driveway, or better yet, catch a glimpse of the King himself strolling the grounds or riding his motorcycle around Memphis. (If you were really lucky, he might give you a pink Cadillac!)

Elvis became so establishment that on a trip to Washington DC in 1970, he dropped by the headquarters of the FBI to volunteer his services as an undercover agent. It seems that Elvis was peeved at the Beatles for their 'filthy, unkempt appearance and suggestive music.' Elvis explained to Research Chief M. A. Jones, who interviewed him, that his own long hair and unusual appearance were mere 'tools of the trade which allowed him access to and rapport with many people.' Imagine that. Here is society's one-time bad boy offering to join the good guys to help stamp out the new-wave child corrupters. Director of the FBI, J. Edgar Hoover, later wrote Elvis a letter telling him he would 'keep in mind your offer to be of assistance.'[4]

Success, the kind Elvis had, goes a long way toward making a person respectable. Now, years after his death, Elvis is a sort of saint, and Graceland Mansion in Memphis is a shrine to tearful pilgrims from all over the world. His life story is told and retold in a stream of films, books and television documentaries.

Some might take the pessimistic view that the very acceptance of Elvis is proof positive of the moral decline this world

_____ *STARMAKER MACHINERY*

is skidding into. Others might argue that we have merely grown up a bit and learned that Elvis was not so bad after all. Elvis certainly was not as evil as he was made out to be in the early days, but he did open the door for some genuinely dangerous influences to come in after him. Others would pick up the cues he laid down and push far beyond his furthest limits.

This indicates a rather frightening progression: the younger members of society come into contact with increasingly rough, ever more malignant influences which face them when they are least able to withstand such forces. Capitulation, in some form, would seem almost inevitable.

However, it should be remembered that rock, though potent, is still only one part of the cultural mix, and that all people are not affected equally by their cultural environment. In fact, the sheer multiplicity of possible influences almost guarantees that whatever influences do reach a person will be somewhat diluted. Also, people do not interpret elements of culture in black and white terms. Always, overt stimuli are filtered through the highly individualized perceptions of the person involved, to be acted on in any of a billion ways. Rarely are influences internalized directly and instantaneously.

maS, niaga ti yalP

And speaking of influence, let's touch briefly on the practice known as 'backward masking' — that is, recording a word, phrase or musical snippet and reversing the tape so that it plays backwards. This backward bit is then added to the final mix of the song as something of a special effect. The Beatles used it in their landmark album, *Sgt. Pepper's Lonely Hearts Club Band*. Since then, it has become a fairly common production device.

But according to some people this device took a particularly nasty turn somewhere along the way when certain rock groups — Led Zeppelin, the Eagles, Blue Oyster Cult, AC/DC, among others —began recording sexual or even satanic messages and dropping them into their songs, backward, underneath the rest of the music. Thus, when the songs are played normally, the sinister message is 'masked' from the listener.

Masked, but not hidden completely, for these backward messages can still be picked up subliminally, thus entering the mind below the level of conscious awareness. Impressionable listeners are subjected to direct and instantaneous influence of a most reprehensible kind. They are indoctrinated without the slightest hint of what is happening...

At least that's the claim. And it has created quite a flap in certain circles. I've received numerous letters from people who've heard about backward masking and are concerned about it, and the subject has come up on radio interviews — including one where I was asked to debate the issue with two people who'd written a book exposing the whole diabolical scheme. (Apparently, they played all their records backwards listening for backward-recorded bits to emerge as regular forward speech.)

But before we get too carried away, let's take a couple of steps back. First of all, is it possible?

Yes, as already mentioned, backward recording is a common production effect. Therefore, anyone who cared to could record whatever message they chose and have it mixed in backwards at virtually any level of audibility. No problem.

Now then, what about the message so recorded? Here's where the theory runs aground.

It has never been satisfactorily explained to me exactly how the brain unscrambles the mass of meaningless sounds that is backward-recorded speech, especially when buried underneath layers and layers of more meaningful sound. By what means is this deciphering accomplished?

Those who believe in backward masking are extremely vague on this point. Presumably, we all have some innate faculty (which needs no explanation): the ability to decode inaudible gibberish.

STARMAKER MACHINERY

I've listened to tapes played backwards, with the sound well up so I wouldn't miss anything, and have never been able to understand a single word — subliminally or otherwise — even when I knew what the people were saying. Or, if my brain did actually decode the scrambled speech subconsciously, it's keeping the message to itself.

The problem lies in the diphthong — that little feature of human speech whereby combined vowels are transmuted into individual sounds, rather than enunciated separately. The word toy, for example, is diphthongized and results in a simple monosyllabic word with an 'oi' sound. Otherwise, I suppose, we would pronounce each vowel individually resulting in a two syllable word pronounce 'toe-ee.' Now, as it happens, diphthongs do not translate backwards.

In other words, when a diphthong is played backwards it loses its peculiar sound. The 'oy' sound of toy is not simply 'yo' because of the way words are aspirated. We can try to say a word backwards, reversing the vowel sound, perhaps, but the resulting word is still aspirated *forwards*. We talk by pushing air up through out vocal cords and out our mouths and not the other way round.

Therefore, for backward masking to work, our clever brains have intuitively to know and understand reversed diphthongs and backwards aspiration — recognizing, decoding, and reversing them in milliseconds. And if that weren't enough this process is carried out with material that is not only inaudible to the human ear, but buried under layers of less subtle, more accessible sound.

But suppose we were able to do just that, suppose that our subconscious minds have nothing better to do while we are listening to music than monitor those auditory circuits capable of hearing subliminal sound, sift out backwards speech, reassemble it and derive its message. Suppose we *were* able to do it? What then?

It all depends on how the subconscious mind reacts to such messages. Do the words 'Satan is lord' (which is the reported message of one of the more notorious examples) in themselves possess any innate power to influence? Because my subconscious mind receives this message, exactly how am I influenced?

The implication is that because this message has bypassed normal information-gathering channels it is somehow more powerful or influential than if I merely read it off a cereal packet. Actually, the whole theory of backward masking rests on this point: those who believe in backward masking believe that these messages *are* more influential, that they actively affect us for the worse.

However, I have always believed (and have been so taught by my spiritual superiors) that the part of me that God works with and is therefore interested in most is the part that is in my direct control — my will, in other words. The part of me that is beyond my conscious control, my subconscious, is just that — beyond my control. Anything beyond human control would seem to be God's concern, not mine.

As a Christian I am responsible only for those things I *can* do something about, those things that reach me on a conscious level. I am not responsible for the things that lie outside my conscious control and influence. I am not responsible for my nightly dreams, for instance, most of which I don't remember anyway. Dreams, I am told, are products of my subconscious mind — and I have never, ever, heard anyone suggest I ought to be in better control of them in one way or another. Of course, when, or *if*, the content of my dreams reaches my conscious mind I can deal with it. But then it isn't subconscious anymore, since I am reacting to it consciously.

Backward masking would seem to fall into the same category as dreams. Even granting that it was somehow possible for backward masking to operate like its believers claim it does — which is granting quite a lot since there has never been any real proof that backward masking was ever performed in the first place (actually, backward masking is just a variation on the whole subliminal motivation theory that started with soft-drink ads being spliced into films, which was never proven, either) — still, allowing the widest possible latitude and supposing that backward masking could speak to the psyche, the individual could not be moved to any particular action until the message reached the conscious level in some way, at which point it would come under interpretation and control of the will — that is, the portion of the human consciousness that determines right and wrong. We aren't zombies after all.

Once under control of the will, it would seem to me, any 'messages of deception' would be acted on in the usual way. And if simply hearing the words 'Satan is lord' influenced people in some ugly and malign way, we'd all be in trouble, for that is, in a word, magic.

Personally, I would be inclined to dismiss the whole backward masking thing as just another of these sensational scare campaigns which appeal to the persecution complex of certain people. In any case, it illustrates quite well the sort of irrationality that sometimes surrounds rock music, and the inability, or perhaps unwillingness, to separate the illusions from reality.

Real tragedy

Those looking for harmful influences in the lives of young people don't have to believe exotic and unproven nonsense like backward masking. The real tragedy is that far too many young people find in pop culture the only value and meaning for their lives.

But in an age when parents, teachers and even church leaders often forsake the responsibility of teaching and modelling wholesome moral values, too many young people are forced to search for direction on their own. Left to their own devices they look to whatever source they can find — friends first and then to whoever meets them on their own ground. For many, since music speaks forcefully to special inner needs, rock stars and rock music can indeed become significant agents in shaping attitudes and defining parameters of belief and behaviour — hardly a comforting thought.

On the other hand, it's worth remembering that strict conformity to an established set of values can always be bought, but the price is high. Young people can be made to mouth the party line or ape a predetermined standard of behaviour — but always at the cost of true maturity. Thus, ridding the world of rock music and rock musicians, as pleasant as that might seem, is not the final solution to helping individuals form healthy moral and spiritual values. Laying down the law, saying, 'Absolutely no more rock music in this house!' is rarely by itself a satisfactory response.

In the end, who determines what influence popular culture has on the individual? The superstars themselves, or the fans that created them? Is morality at the mercy of ephemeral style-mongers, or is it more directly shaped by the everyday attitudes of a much wider, more varied and complex society? Is there finally some latent moral ethic engraved on humanity which keeps it from degenerating completely into savagery with each new generation?

The illusions of rock make it seem more powerful, more pervasive than it really is, and much more persuasive. But the Top 40 is a dizzy merry-go-round; every week, year in, year out, the charts record the rise and fall of each pop performer's fortunes. The sway of any one group or individual is brief, measured in days — a hit one day, a has-been the next, as the spotlight of public attention races on.

▶ chapter 4

The heart of rock

Rock and its beat ▶

ROCK ON TRIAL

Rock 'n' roll streaked in on Haley's Comets in 1955 to the tune of 'Rock Around the Clock.' Before that there had been rhythm and blues, boogie, bop, swing, New Orleans jazz, blues and ragtime, stretching back in an unbroken chain to the dark jungles of Africa where the 'beat' was originally conceived centuries before.

There, in frenzied displays of pagan ritual, tribes of naked, sweating savages pounded out their jungle rhythms under the mesmerizing stare of demon idols. Inspired by evil and nurtured in sin, the beat flourished on the dark continent until it was transplanted to the shores of America with the slaves.

At least, that's one popular notion of rock's history.

The African Connection is something in which many well intentioned citizens and self-appointed rock historians put a great deal of faith. It's a serviceable myth, but is there any truth in it?

▶ *Problem: Rock has a strong, compelling beat. It is very dangerous since it owes its beginnings to African demon worship and may itself be demon inspired.*

The problem points to the apparent similarities between rock and some of Africa's tribal music. There is no question that music is, and probably always has been, an important part

THE HEART OF ROCK

of the lives of the African peoples. But the connection between the music of various African tribes, America's slaves and the rock music of today is tenuous at best.

Slavery in America was more than an embarrassing historical fact. Men, women and children were ripped from their homes and families and stuffed into ships as cargo bound for the land of liberty. Upon their arrival, any surviving slaves were sold on the auction block in various ports in America.

These native African slaves brought with them certain aspects of their culture: folklore, religion, language, traditions and music. But after living and working in the New World for a few decades, Blacks saw they were never going to get back home and began adopting the culture of their captors, becoming more Western in their thinking and living. And if they did not choose to make the adjustment on their own initiative, it was often chosen for them by owners who wanted 'civilized' slaves.

Some rock historians unwittingly suggest that although they spoke English and considered themselves American, the slaves' music remained outside the Americanization process. Black music, they say, developed into a number of distinct styles — spirituals, blues, ragtime, jazz — and somehow managed to retain that old black magic in the beat. That is where the trouble is, they say — in the beat. The 'Black beat,' we are told, is an evil beat because it was developed in music used in heathen worship.

The basic premise is that rock music can be linked directly to the forms of music used by Blacks for heathen worship.

Bob Larson, antirock crusader, said in his book *The Day Music Died*, 'In America, rock music has its roots in jazz — an emotional music which gives vent to feelings — and in Negro gospel singing from which the rhythm and blues come.' He then goes on to link the American Black with its mythical past. 'It is probably incidental (though some might cite scriptural references otherwise) that the black man has fostered the music which at one time incited heathens to frenzy and cannibalism.'[1]

Rock's roots

Africa is a very big place. It has more than three times the area of the United States and even more geographical diversity. It also contains over five thousand separate peoples with perhaps as many different cultures, languages and religions.

Various European countries captured slaves from outlets all along the coasts of Africa. Most of the slaves who found their way to the United States came not from the tropical rain forests but from the northern regions of the great savannas, the area of Nigeria and the Ivory Coast. Interestingly, the drum (and therefore, 'the beat') was not an important instrument in the northern region of Africa. Tony Palmer, in *All You Need Is Love: The Story of Popular Music*, observes, 'The principal musical instruments of the savanna were stringed...Particularly common was the *banya*.' The *banya* is the father of today's banjo. Palmer also points out that the banya did not originate in Africa, but came there by way of Egyptian caravans.[2]

Any drums such as the slaves might have possessed were prohibited by white slaveholders in America because plantation owners believed (perhaps rightly so, perhaps not) that the messages of revolt could be passed back and forth between groups of slaves. The banjo, on the other hand, had a brighter future as the slaves' chief musical instrument since its usefulness as a telephone was almost nil.

As Palmer observes, 'Drums were almost never heard in black American music until well into the twentieth century.' That is, of course, well after the emergence of jazz, blues and spirituals.[3]

Africa has contributed a great deal to American music. But musical influences are not easy to unravel; clear lines for tracing music back into uncharted history are not as neatly laid out as some think. Some music historians such

THE HEART OF ROCK

as George Pullen Jackson discredit the African connection completely by suggesting that American Blacks learned their music from the Whites. Bruno Nettl in *Music in Primitive Culture* states that 'Jackson has traced the history of the spiritual (forerunner of jazz and the blues) and has concluded that it originated in the Scotch-Irish and English hymnody of the South.... He traced Negro spirituals to white hymnbooks of the nineteenth century and concludes that Negroes learned the hymns from the Whites.'[4]

The belief that 'the beat' stayed alive or even existed in the music of the slaves rests on a shaky foundation. It is difficult to support the idea that Black music survived in America (with no important changes) when everything else of African culture, such as language, customs, dress and religion, was either forbidden, abandoned or forgotten. One could make a more convincing case that the rock beat came from country-western music since the first rock songs were played and recorded by a country swing band originally known as 'The Saddlemen.' Under Bill Haley's leadership, this group (later known as the Comets) as we have seen, got rock rolling. Haley was not Black, played no jazz and came from New York.

Much that has been written against rock music in this area is actually disguised racial hatred: racism. The words used to describe it display this fact — 'jungle music,' 'black boogie,' 'demon beat' and so on. There was a time when Whites discouraged rock 'n' roll shows for the simple fact that they drew both Black and White audiences. Concerned parents did not, to put it mildly, want their children mixing with racially different children.

As for the charge that rock's rhythm is demon inspired, most people overlook the obvious fact that in other places where New World slaves landed (Jamaica, Haiti, the islands of the West Indies) nothing close to rock music ever evolved. If the beat was so powerful and so much a part of the musical make-up of these people, why didn't rock develop in the Caribbean as well? Or, to put it the other way around, why

ROCK ON TRIAL

don't calypso or reggae, the popular musical styles of the islands, utilize the same rhythms?

That rock and its 'evil beat' originated with the slaves of Africa is a racist notion which will not stand up. About all that can be said is this: the music which for many years has been associated with Blacks in America emerged out of the general soup of America's mixing cultures where creative influences are infinite. Jazz, like rhythm and blues, ragtime and the rest which are so often considered the property of Blacks, were formed in the give-and-take of many cultural backgrounds (German, Czech, French, Irish, English and others) over many years. Even the music of Africa is not purely indigenous. It was shaped by its contact with Europe, Asia and the Middle East. To lay the origins of a music condemned for its savagery and immorality at the feet of one racial group shows a narrow interpretation of history. Worse, it is an insidious form of prejudice and racism which should be condemned, not indulged.

'But even if the rock beat did not originate with Black Africans, it's still evil,' claim rock's critics. 'The rock beat short-circuits the mind and excites men and women's baser instincts. Subjection to such powerful rhythms can cause great harm mentally, physically and emotionally.'

The beat goes on and on...

Like every living thing on this planet, humans are rhythmic beings. We are affected by the constant ebb and flow of life's forces: sunrise, sunset; the changing seasons; monthly and yearly cycles. Especially critical are the rhythms of our heartbeat and breathing which continue moment by moment throughout our life.

The 'evil' beat in question is the notorious *syncopated* beat, also called a backbeat. Syncopation is a simple musical device, and a common one at that, used in a variety of musical styles including church music (such as Luther's original 'A mighty fortress'). Syncopation is merely the accenting of a beat between the regular beats of the rhythm.

THE HEART OF ROCK

You might call it misplacing the beat. It works like this: if the regular beat goes 1-2-3-4, syncopating it might make it go 1-and-2-and-3-and-4. Say it to yourself emphasizing the 'and,' and you will get some idea of what is happening.

Most, but by no means all, rock music is written in regular 4/4 time. Syncopating the beat makes it more interesting to play and listen to. Classical music also uses syncopation, such as Stravinsky's well-known 'Firebird Suite,' Beethoven's early work and much of Schumann's. It is a device often used to spice up long passages or provide an interesting change of pace. However, since the rhythms of classical music are not as prominent as they are in rock, a listener may not as easily notice when syncopation is used. Of course, not all rock is syncopated, but since rock is a music of few elements, the beat is very close to the surface and is easily apprehended.

All musical rhythm is based on the idea of anticipation. As the music unfolds, the listener's mind reviews the pattern of beats that make up the rhythm, and projects or anticipates the beats to follow. When the anticipated beat follows as expected, the listener is satisfied. Syncopation breaks up this process. The accented beat is different from what is anticipated. This is what makes rock feel jerky or impulsive to those unaccustomed to its eccentricities.

The contention of some is that this truncated beat is harmful to the human organism because it upsets the natural balance, or rhythm, of the body or mind.

In the late sixties, when hard rock was at its height, many people, including physicians, psychologists, sociologists and educators, became concerned about the effects which loud noise and powerful rhythms might have on young people. Experiments were designed, samples were taken, studies were conducted, and the evidence sifted for hard facts. Some investigations were scientific and honest; others were careless and spurious.

One of the more famous tests involved three groups of plants. The plants in Plot A got good healthy doses of classical music beamed at them all day long. Plant Plot B was bombarded relentlessly with hard rock. Plant Plot C was a control group that heard only the sounds of Mother Nature herself.

The results? Plot A developed a strong affinity for classical music and grew in the direction of the speakers. Plot C grew straight and tall as average plants do. But Plot B, subjected to hard rock, first turned away from the speakers and then sickened and died.

Whether this test was actually carried out, or whether it is just a modern folk tale passed around and augmented by whoever picks it up — like the eyewitness accounts of giant albino alligators that inhabit the sewers of New York City — is really secondary. What is significant is that it represents a certain mindset which eagerly accepts any fact or example, as long as it is 'scientific,' to prove a point. (One source attributes a similar experiment to a Mrs Dorothy Retallack, a housewife from Denver, Colorado, who could kill her house plants in four weeks with a steady diet of Led Zeppelin and Vanilla Fudge. Of course, that was in the sixties.)

On the strength of absurd association alone, the plant plot test hopes to make us think, 'If rock music can do that to plants, just imagine what it does to people!' However, even assuming the test was real, the results tell nothing about human beings, or rock music. It says nothing in particular about plants either. A careful scientist would never draw such conclusions or allow such a vaguely constructed test to answer hard questions.

Music *does* affect people. Musicians and their audiences have always known this. Long before rock came along, doctors were studying the uses of music in treating people physically and psychologically. They found that music played in factories could help people work more efficiently, that mental patients slept better and fought with each other less when music was played over the public address system. Today's supermarkets, dentists' offices, airline terminals and elevators all have their own brand of music for their own therapeutic purposes. Dentists play soothing music to help calm people's fears; supermarkets hope to create a cheerful atmosphere where people feel good about spending money.

In fact, the emotional influence of music has been carefully documented in tests conducted by psychologists in the early 1930s. A psychologist named Hevener explored the whole spectrum of human emotion from joyful, playful and aggressive, to mournful, yearning and depressed — using classical music entirely. She found that even people untrained in music could intelligently and accurately describe their feelings as they listened to various pieces of music.

Other psychologists and musicologists devised a number of tests to determine the physical and emotional sensitivity of listeners to music and their awareness of its effects on them. The research found that while people were sensitive, they were also quite aware of what the music was doing to them emotionally. They were, if asked, able to give quite detailed and objective statements about their feelings. In other words, although people were emotionally influenced by music, they were not dominated by it. Their feelings were always monitored by the mind. Those listening knew what they were feeling; there were not influenced without knowing it.[5]

Objective research challenges the notion that rock seizes a person's mind or otherwise takes control, a notion which Bob Larson epitomized when he stated, 'It is quite obvious to any qualified, objective observer that teenagers dancing to rock music often enter hypnotic trances. When control of the mind is weakened or lost, evil influences can often take possession. Loss of self-control is dangerous and sinful. In a state of hypnosis the mind of the listener can respond to almost any suggestion given to it.'[6]

Is rock hypnotic? Really? The notions of loss of control and zombielike trances are popular misconceptions played up by Hollywood and stage hypnotists, but far removed from the real thing. Dr William Kroger, a pioneer in the use of clinical hypnosis in medical therapy, has for over forty years taught the basic principles of hypnosis to more than one hundred thousand physicians throughout the world. He describes hypnosis as simply a process of relaxation, 'whereby, because you relax better, you hear better. And whenever you hear better, whatever I say to you or whatever you say to yourself will "sink in" better. If it sinks in better, you will respond better. This allows greater awareness. Since you are more aware, you naturally cannot be asleep. You go into a superalert state whenever you desire and you come out of it whenever you wish. You are always in control.'[7]

Hypnosis is a state of alert concentration involving relaxation. Hypnotized people are fully aware and in control of themselves and their thoughts at all time. They have more control, not less.

Concentration, relaxation — two postures difficult to create or maintain at a rock concert. And what of this extreme vulnerability to suggestion which has been described? Even stage magicians know that subjects under hypnosis cannot be made to do anything against their own will — that is, anything they would not do when not hypnotized. Thus, people do not become mindless automatons, whether responding to a hypnotist's suggestion or in subjection to the so-called hypnotic powers of rock music.

But looking at the way people jump around at rock concerts, one might think it was the music whipping everyone into a frenzy. It is a mildly logical assumption. But better evidence indicates the simple fact that people jump and gyrate, leap around and lose control because they *want* to. Rock frenzies, like sport stadium frenzies or summer clearance sale frenzies, are self-induced, not rhythm induced, and each participant can choose how to react. Music does have power to move, but not to override normal sensibilities.

It is telling that what made people scream and faint in

the sixties fails to elicit anything but a snicker today. Watch a film of the Beatles at Shea Stadium, the stands packed with thousands of screeching, crying fans, and you wonder what all the commotion was about. Was it the music? No, if the music was the mover, those bouncy songs would still drive people crazy. Put on a stack of old Beatles records today and you won't get anybody to scream and tear their hair. It's out of style. They don't *want* to do it.

So, what's the bottom line, beatwise? We know (1) syncopation is a common musical device used in a variety of musical styles with no particularly abnormal effects on people; (2) all music affects people emotionally but does not short-circuit the normal mental processes; and, thus (3) rock music is not hypnotic. Any apparent loss of control is self-induced by enthusiastic listeners and limited to the immediate popularity of the performer or the atmosphere surrounding the performance. People are not emotionally or psychologically damaged by exposure to rock beats and are not seized or otherwise overpowered by rock rhythms against their will.

A beat or rhythm is not evil. The very fact that rhythm is a universal part of all existence should show us that it is a natural part of our lives and not something to be feared or condemned. Rock may use stronger or more urgent rhythms than other forms of music, but since all music uses rhythm, the issue becomes a question of degree or intensity.

Some suggest that when the beat becomes the main focus of the music, overwhelming all other components, that is when the trouble begins. The pulsating beat assaults the mind and puts it to sleep, so to speak, opening it to the evil invasion while the listener is off guard. That is the assertion.

But how is such a statement to be proven? Or disproven? The argument at that point moves from the realm of the concrete to the metaphysical. And metaphysical arguments cannot be settled in the laboratory, or someone's flower garden.

While it may be possible to show that under certain conditions the mind may enter an altered state of consciousness, does it necessarily follow that evil forces automatically invade when normal attention is diminished or changed? On what grounds is that to be believed? It is pure conjecture on the part of people who have other axes to grind. The point is that the interplay between the physical, mental, emotional and spiritual aspects of human beings are extremely complex, and questions of how this elaborate interplay works or can be influenced are not likely to be neatly elucidated by any single theory or notion, even a religious one.

Help me, Dr Feelgood

No, rock music cannot take you anywhere you do not want to go. However, it can make it easier for you to go somewhere you do want to go but know you shouldn't. This has nothing to do with rhythm or beat, hypnotic or otherwise. This 'grease on the slide to depravity' is supplied by the general cultural atmosphere surrounding rock music — the way the performers and the fans themselves live.

Rock is seen as a Dr Feelgood, the lighthearted healing agent that slaps happy-face Band-Aids on the various emotional bruises of its fans. This is one of rock's most attractive and influential guises, seemingly harmless on the surface. But isn't there more to it than that?

chapter 5
Lyrically speaking

Rock and its message

'A wave of vulgar, filthy and suggestive music has inundated the land...It is artistically and morally depressing and should be suppressed by press and pulpit.'[1]

This journalistic judgement reflects a common view about rock music. However, the above snippet came from an American magazine called the *Musical Courier*, and the music which so outraged the writer was a slick, fast-paced, jumpy music called ragtime. The year was 1899 and ragtime was the rage, and by most accounts the state of the union was morally bankrupt.

Morality, it seems, is always taking it on the chin in America.

▶ *Problem: Rock music is a rough music, dealing with the lower side of human nature. It creates an unhealthy mental environment for its listeners through suggestive lyrics and obscene connotations. Rock excites a person's sexual drives and projects an atmosphere where immorality is acceptable.*

It seems a curious fact of history that each new generation thinks itself the first and the older generation thinks it the worst. Of course it is neither. History is crowded with examples where certain greybeards have shaken their heads, predicting the downfall of the world over this or that newfangled invention. And the steady erosion of morality at the hands of popular entertainers is a timeworn theme.

This is a universal trend noted by John Rublowsky in his book *Popular Music*. 'It is hard to believe that the waltz was considered scandalous when it was first introduced at the end of the eighteenth century.' Polite society refused to condone such a barbaric dance. Their music was the minuet, much more 'refined.' But despite prevailing opinion, 'the minuet was replaced and the waltz became respectable.'[2]

Years later, jazz was named as the cause of horrendous moral lapses. *Ladies Home Journal* put the question like this: 'Does Jazz Put the Sin in Syncopation?' and also championed the cry, 'Unspeakable Jazz Must Go!' Some anonymous busybody traced the moral decline and fall of a thousand girls in Chicago from 1920 to 1922 directly to jazz. Women were reported to leap onto tables and tear off their clothes while screaming in ecstasy as the Original Dixieland Jazz Band raced through its paces. America's youth were thought to be in serious peril from the creeping menace.

Twenty years later it was a new peril and the menace was named Frankie, as in Sinatra. 'Swoonatraism' was sweeping many countries, especially among bobby-soxed females aged fourteen. 'His cigarette butts, his uneaten cornflakes became highly prized items. So did locks of his hair, often plucked from his very head. The hysteria was compared to the Children's Crusade of the Middle Ages.'[3]

The wheels of style revolve slowly onward, changing with the times. However, certain themes remain the same: sex is a perennial favourite.

Sex in song is not new. Every age has had its bawdy songs, illicit lyrics, *double entendres* conveyed through metrical rhyme. Rock music is no exception, and from this point of view it stands guilty; sexuality of all kinds is expressed in rock music. Popular music, including rock, has a way of expressing what is on the minds of its writers and listeners, the basic thoughts and feelings of human beings. When people have sex on their minds, it comes out in a song.

ROCK ON TRIAL

Most popular songs (of any era) are of the boy-meets/loses/marries-girl type: innocent, sugarcoated, inoffensive sentiments. Rock has this side, but often its expressions are stronger, earthier; it is a forceful music, and the words it chooses are forceful, too.

It could be argued that there is more blatant sexual immorality being peddled in popular music now than ever before; I believe this is true. There is also more explicit sexuality displayed in films, books, television and magazines as part of the growing permissiveness of society.

I would suggest that music, although clearly part of the problem, is *not* the sole cause. The problem of blatant, inappropriate or perverse sexual matter is much bigger than rock music itself. That does not excuse rock for its part in the mess, but it should clue critics to the fact that burning piles of rock records in church car parks will not reverse the trend.

Like television shows and films that rely heavily on sex to sell themselves, music of any type that indulges itself in the same way should be condemned. But should all rock music be banned because of the excesses of some songs? That is hardly fair.

Rock and the vigilantes

Suppose for a moment that a group of vigilantes were to rise up and take it upon themselves to rid society of all media that foist morally questionable material on the public. Rock, of course, would be among the first to go. But to be thorough and consistent this group would have to go to bat against television programmes like 'Dallas' and 'Dynasty,' magazines of all types (not just those obviously pornographic), advertisements in all mediums, films and books of all types. Many chat show hosts would have to be taken off the air. To reform all the areas mentioned would be a Herculean task indeed. But suppose the vigilantes did the job on contemporary cultural media. Then what?

Consider the classics. *Oedipus the King*, one of the most widely read of the classic Greek plays, centres around the dual theme of incest and murder. Homer's brave Odysseus played the crafty culprit of a host of crimes ranging from fornication to theft to murder. Oedipus and Odysseus are introduced to thirteen-year-old children in many school systems.

And what about classical music? Perhaps because classical music's image is propriety itself, most people would not think of reforming it in any way. In fact, classical music is sometimes suggested as an antidote to rock music. Yet classical music, especially opera, often deals in rank immorality. Murder, adultery, rape, promiscuity, revenge, graft, corruption in high places are all part of the operatic tradition.

Die Fledermaus, by Johann Strauss, one of the best-loved comic operas, is the story of lover-swapping singles. The action takes place at a ball given by homosexual Prince Orlovsky whose main aria invites his guests to make love, 'each to his own taste.' It sounds more like the plot of a video nasty than a genteel nineteenth-century work of art.

Wagner, universally recognized as one of the world's truly great composers, was a megalomaniac within reach of lunacy. He was grossly immoral, selfish, adulterous, arrogant, wildly hedonistic and violently racist. He was a thief to boot. Yet Wagner's works are performed today throughout the major concert venues of the world. There seems to be little concern that they were composed by a man of indisputably immoral character.

In a book on classical music released by a Christian publisher, an entire section devoted to Wagner manages to downplay the sin this man wallowed in throughout his sordid life. With a bare hint at the truth, the book innocently mentions that Wagner was 'inconsiderate, self-obsessed, and melancholy'[4] — which is like saying Jack the Ripper was a cad unsociable with the ladies. In truth, Wagner was a man rabidly anti-Christian and anti-Jewish. He was much admired by Hitler, who found in Wagner a kindred spirit, and in his music a way to stoke the German war machine.

ROCK ON TRIAL

Classical music has much that would condemn it from a strictly moralistic standpoint, whether in the subject matter or in the lives of its composers. Yet to consign classical recordings to the flames would strike most of us as barbaric. We are brought up to regard classical music as the highest expression of musical art. Burning a few rock records, on the other hand, seems like an appropriate demonstration, despite the fact that the contents of any random rock record may actually be less offensive than the typical opera.

Recently a group in the USA known as the Washington Wives, alarmed by some of the things they were hearing on the radio and on their turntables at home, made headlines by sponsoring an informal congressional investigation into the problem of filthy rock lyrics and rallying support for a record album rating system to rate rock records the same way America's films are rated — G for inoffensive, R for racy, X for excessively smutty and so on.

The members of congress who assembled for the probe heard testimony from rock musicians and record industry spokespersons and concluded vaguely that the women had a point, and that something ought to be done to protect the innocent and that perhaps a rating system made good sense.

The problem with rating a record in this way is that, human nature being what it is, the R's and X's of the rock world will suddenly look a whole lot more attractive for being branded. Curiosity alone will fuel increased listening activity by youngsters. As soon as marginal artists discover they can increase sales by spicing up the lyrics or the album cover and trying for an R or X rating for their albums, they'll go out of their way to do so. Legitimate artists may even feel the need to include some smut in order to compete, or to have their music taken seriously. A G-rated album will become a rarity, a thing of the past, just like G-rated movies — not through any artistic inhibition, but due to inevitable commercial pressures. PG and R movies make money; a G rating is the kiss of death, financial suicide.

Then again, who will administrate the rating system? Will

it rate only rock records, or will the country and western, blues, jazz and easy listening sections of the record bins come under the rating system, too? And why stop with records? Why not go whole hog and start rating books and TV programmes? How about clothing styles, or magazine ads?

In presenting the inconsistencies of our culture and the casual tolerance of immorality in many other forms, my purpose is not to condone rock music's excesses or defend them in any way. I am not saying immorality in music is right because it is accepted or that because we accept casual immorality in many other areas of our lives we should accept it in rock music as well. My purpose has been to put the problem into perspective.

Where rock music is concerned, the problem is clearly not so much the perception of immorality as music appreciation. The classical music buff is not long bothered that Wagner hated Jews, indulged in orgies or stole the wife of his conductor. Wagner's music is still appreciated for what it is. The question of music appreciation is considered more fully in chapter ten but, as we have seen already, it is a matter of culture and taste. We grow up accepting classical music and think highly of it (whether or not we actually understand or listen to it) because our culture assures us it is worthy. The cultural trend toward the acceptance of rock as a legitimate artistic style is under way. Will rock ever hold the same high regard reserved for the classical arts? Time alone will tell.

Tunnel vision

Rock is characterized by some as expressing only sex-, drug- or anarchy-related themes. While it is true that there have been plenty of rock songs grouped around those themes, the range of expression in rock is actually quite wide.

That fact can be simply demonstrated by looking at a popular song chart. Among the typical boy/girl romantic musings are songs which explore basic human sentiments (loneliness, vulnerability, genuine love or the absence of it, sanctity of human life), modern concerns (the emptiness of transitory relationships, the drive for success, facing old age), political and social issues (world peace, hunger, racism, the brutality of urban life) and lifestyle questions (simple living and rediscovering honest, worthwhile values).

In the midst of these laudable themes, you'll also find expression of two of this century's most ruthless and damaging philosophies: secular humanism and nihilism. Briefly stated, secular humanism is that branch of thought which affirms the dignity and worth of humanity and its capacity for self-realization through reason alone, rejecting any supernatural or spiritual considerations. Nihilism asserts the dismal view that traditional values, morals and beliefs are unfounded, that society's present condition is so irredeemably hopeless that annihilation may be preferable to any positive attempt to save it. After all, existence is meaningless anyway.

Secular humanism is the darling of the moment; almost all modern literature, drama, films and music espouse the view consciously or unconsciously that 'we're all we've got,' and furthermore, that we're enough. The heroes of stage and story are trotted before us to face inhuman obstacles, often with supreme courage, unshakeable conviction and self-sacrificing love — all without a mention that we might draw strength or comfort from our Creator, or that we even have a Creator who stands above human efforts. This is insidious, subtle and damning.

Ultimately, secular humanism shades off into nihilism because myopic good faith cannot forever withstand the terrible onslaught of reality: we are lost without God! Lost in every sense of the word. When the humanists realize this, they throw themselves into the bottomless pit of eternal despair. For after denying spiritual needs and never admitting God's active, redeeming presence, from where is salvation to come?

Of course, none of this is presented overtly; the message

is usually far more subtle. But when was the last time you watched a television programme, even a 'family' programme, which remotely suggested that the protagonist's problems might have spiritual solutions or that the hero may at some later date be haunted by the moral implications of his it-seemed-like-the-thing-to-do-at-the-time actions?

Here is the real dilemma of the modern age — not sex, drugs or rebellion. Those are merely blemishes, the symptoms of a raging, deadly disease. To treat the symptoms without properly diagnosing the disease is to attempt to hold back an onrushing tidal wave with nothing but a mop and powerful good intentions.

The disease is real. It has touched the very core of human life on this planet and now everything suffers — the way we think, the way we act, our relationships, the books we read, the music we listen to. The disease has contaminated everything of value. Rock music is just one more avenue of human endeavour which has been contaminated by secular humanism. The cure does not lie in closing off all contaminated avenues, be they rock or literature or theatre. The disease will still remain. The cure lies in combating the disease directly.

▶ chapter 6
Every picture tells a story

Rock and music videos ▶

ROCK ON TRIAL

In the late seventies, rock music, which had for more than twenty-five years moved from strength to strength, conquering new worlds almost every other week, suddenly went limp in the sales department. Record companies, bloated and sated by years of easy pickings, awakened with alarm to the sight of all their gold turning to lead. The lethargic giants scratched their heads and muttered dark curses against a sluggish economy, skyrocketing oil prices (record vinyl is derived from oil) and a villainous public that stole their wares via cassette recorder over stereo FM rather than pay for the product at the record shop.

The downward trend continued into the eighties. While executive heads rolled, everything from recording budgets to staff fringe benefits, and even the staff itself, was cut in an effort to stay in the game. Meanwhile everyone searched for something, anything, to save their collective bacon.

They found it in an unlikely place: television. For years TV had been looked upon with outright distrust by most people in the business of rock music. It was thought, perhaps rightly so, that television was bad for rock and pop music.

Most in the record business recognized the close, almost sacred, connection between a recording artist's personal performances and record sales. Artists built an audience by touring, kept and maintained their audience by touring, and it was thought that people did not pay hard-earned cash to see in person performers they could see for free on the tube. TV devalued the goods, in other words, by oversaturation.

But suddenly minds were changing. What changed them? Rock videos.

Rock videos, music videos, or just plain 'videos,' as they are most often called, are those surrealistic minifilms shown on late-night TV (or twenty-four hours a day if you happen to subscribe to certain satellite channels). As films, however, they exist solely to promote their soundtracks — the song they are designed to feature.

Record companies found in rock video their salvation, and the downward slide was reversed. Almost overnight rock was back in the driver's seat and rolling again, cruising through the cultural landscape. Music videos gave the music industry a potent sales tool and the business went to work with a will.

But, as is so often the case where rock music is concerned, some people tuned in and became alarmed at what rock music was doing on the tube. 'Disgusting! Violent! Immoral!' carped the critics, and once again there was trouble in paradise.

▶ *Problem: Rock videos go beyond merely setting images to music; they actively interpret the music, trading on the sensual, hedonistic, antihuman aspects of rock and giving it visual emphasis.*

In 1964, at the zenith of their enormous popularity, the Beatles released *A Hard Day's Night* — the film. The film was a lighthearted satire on the Beatles themselves, purporting to follow the Fab Four through a typical day in their charmed lives. It was shot by director Richard Lester in black and white, using a documentary style and featuring numerous Beatle songs. The whole film was shot in just six weeks because the studio and record company wanted to get it into circulation before the 'Merry Mop Tops'' audience magnetism began to wane, as they were certain it would.

The result is a wonderfully daffy picture, crisp, clean and full of fun, as were the Beatles at the time. Although it didn't win the Academy Award for Best Picture that year, in all likelihood it will go down in history for future trivia buffs as the father of rock video.

The idea of linking sound to pictures, despite the creative boost lent by the Beatles, had been kicking around since the invention of 'talkies.' In 1934, German animator Oskar Fischinger orchestrated a ballet of coloured geometrical shapes for a 'Composition in Blue.' Walt Disney had a fling with *Fantasia* in much the same way. A few years later 'soundies' were introduced to bolster the burgeoning interest in jazz of the 1940s, with the likes of Nat King Cole singing 'Frim Fram Sauce.'

Others dabbled with short films along the way, often using film as a substitute for personal appearances — a way to keep a recording artist before the public without mounting an extensive world tour. Usually these shorts were just clips, visual romps with the star clowning for the camera. They were shown in cinemas as support films (remember support films?) or on TV programmes like 'American Bandstand' and 'Top of the Pops.'

Then along came the British band Queen, a group that had been sparring with success for a few years before recording the hit 'Bohemian Rhapsody' in 1977. Along with the song they released a visual presentation which features the group singing the song in different settings — in the studio and clips of live performances — with a few visual tricks thrown in. The first modern rock video was born.

On the strength of their video, Queen's eclectic little tune rocketed to the top of the British charts and planted itself in the Number One spot where it reigned for a phenomenal nine weeks (for ever, in pop music terms), a feat surpassed only once. Behold! A new era in rock promotion was begun.

A good music video, like a good commercial (which it is and more), can sell a song like nothing else. Ask the best-selling recording artist of all time, Mr Pop Music himself, Michael Jackson.

Jackson's mega-monster album *Thriller* was a certified hit the day it hit the streets, quickly selling two million copies. But upon the release of his first video, 'Billie Jean,' the album's sales leaped up to an astonishing ten million copies. The video 'Beat It' followed, keeping the pot boiling. The album had been out a year and was selling a brisk 200,000 copies per week in America when the lavish (fifteen minutes long and costing over a million dollars to produce) 'Thriller' video was beamed to television sets all over the world. Within only five days sales had tripled to a breathtaking 600,000 per week.

The album went on to sell more copies than any other record in music history. Period. End of story. (Over forty-three million copies worldwide at last count.) No-one doubts that Michael Jackson owes a generous portion of the album's success to the spellbinding choreography displayed on those videos, and to TV music programmes like 'Top of the Pops' for turning the broadcast of those videos into media events.

By mid-1983 the power of the music video to promote and sell was clearly established. If any doubters remained, their whines were silenced by the thunderous clatter of pounding feet rushing to produce bigger and better videos.

Seeing is believing

Here is what happened: record companies put their money in video tape, cranking out more and more three-minute commercials. This had the curious side-effect of removing the music further and further from its man-in-the-street appeal (rock as the music of the masses), and restricting the music itself. Since video was important (because video could sell records), it became important for recording artists not only to write commercial music, but to be able to cavort in front of the camera in a convincing manner. New groups had to have the *visuals* as well as the *audios*.

Videos are expensive, too, and so the lists were trimmed

of marginal acts and artists of a more limited appeal in order to free up money for the solid sellers. And even artists with platinum initials were forced into the game since the acts getting all the attention were those with videos. 'Hey, did you see the new Pet Shop Boys video?' 'Yeah, wild. I'm going to get the album.'

No-one seemed to mind that less music was available — there was still an awful lot to go around. No-one seemed to mind that pop music had slipped its philosophical anchor and drifted away from its mass appeal mythos by redefining itself in élitist terms, the province of the few and the fortunate.

But there were some who looked at their TV screens and became disturbed about what they saw. And well they might. Listening to music is one thing, seeing it interpreted graphically is another kettle of fish altogether — a distinctly nasty one, too, when the level of interpretation remains consistently low (as in vulgar), often betraying a decidedly vicious, antihuman side.

Taken as a whole — which is relatively easy to do since they are short and merge quickly into one another — music videos often display a bleak, joyless, hedonistic world, devoid of human warmth and virtue — love, honour, truth, beauty — and one which sports few creature comforts, since what isn't hi-tech chrome-and-glass interiors, is dark alleys or post-holocaust desert.

'Designer violence,' one critic called it. *Designer*, because it all has a slick, chic, commercial look (commercial because many of the directors of rock videos are directors of television commercials); *violence*, because of the casual brutality of it.

And not only do videos flirt with violent images, they actually do violence — to the imagination. Music is an aural experience and a song heard is interpreted privately by the person hearing it. Songs conjure their own special images for each individual. But with music video, the song is pre-interpreted. A meaning is assigned to it by the images of the video, thereby robbing the individual of his own imaginative input — once you have seen the video, its images become your images, its interpretation the *only* interpretation.

On the face of it, this may not seem like a major theft — this hijacking of the individual's imagination. but it is one of the more disturbing side effects of music videos. For when people are prevented from entertaining their own private vision of what the music means, and instead are force-fed a stream of bright, dazzling, often arresting, but basically antihuman images, the human imagination, to say nothing of the human spirit, is cheapened, degraded.

Something lost, something gained

One could argue that music videos should not be considered as music at all, but only as video — an art form in the same category as films. No-one is particularly bothered by the fact that a film interprets its subject for the viewer, leaving little to the imagination — unlike what a book will do. Films are not books, even though so many are based on books; one cannot complain that they don't allow the same kind of imaginative participation as books.

But then again films are not designed with the end in mind of *selling* books. Music videos are — designed for selling records, that is. Videos might share certain characteristics with motion pictures as an art form, but it is only in the sense that magazine advertisements share common characteristics with serious literature.

Others might quibble with this line of argument, pointing out that videos only do, more or less, what musical theatre or film musicals have always done — that is, provide an attractive setting for a song, a pleasing showcase, a treat for the eye as well as the ear.

Nevertheless, it should also be pointed out that videos are, as they say in the data-processing business, 'accessed' differently. Since they are of short duration — three minutes as opposed to two-plus hours for the typical musical —

videos are meant to be viewed repeatedly, and are. Also, musicals do not actually seek to interpret a song so much as showcase it, usually with a dance number. But many music videos do merely that — simply showcase a song, often with stock footage of the artists in concert, or on a studio stage surrounded by high-kicking dancers. A good many others, however, provide what amounts to a mini-film in which the song becomes the soundtrack, providing the narrative for the film. Songs being what they are — with their verse-verse-chorus-verse-bridge-chorus-repeat chorus-fade-out construction — this narrative must be made to fit into a fairly restrictive structure.

Videos have found several ways around this limitation. One is to simply ignore the narrative implied by the lyric and make up another, perhaps more satisfactory one. Another is to fix on a particular element in the lyric, or suggested by it, and expand that into some sort of narrative. A third way is to take a more abstract approach, letting the lyric suggest a theme and then using images to evoke a mood; the images may or, more likely, may not have anything directly to do with the song or its lyric, but are used to reinforce an idea or emotion.

Judging from its prevalence, this last way to turn a song into a soundtrack is the most popular — partly because it offers more creative possibilities, and partly because it's simply easier. Don't worry about what the song says, just put some arresting images on the screen and let the music play. In this way, videos are divorced from any strict narrative responsibility. Narrative implies a story (however minimal), which in turn implies sequential logic. Freed from providing narrative interpretation, videos create meaning (however minimal) by way of what is called 'parallel logic.'

Parallel logic can be quite confusing (not to say disturbing) to some people as it often has a distinctly surreal cast to it. Typically what happens is that the song's lyric suggests one thing while the images presented on the screen suggest something else so that the meaning or interpretation of the song emerges as a hybrid cross between two or more themes, narratives or moods.

This in itself is not necessarily a bad thing. But what makes this potentially unsettling for people is that we human beings invariably seek meaning not only from real-life events, but from the images we see on the various screens around us. Whether we do this out of some innate need to understand our world or merely out of habit is beside the point. The point is people can become disturbed when this quest for meaning is thwarted or discouraged. Parallel logic discourages any attempt to seek meaning in the usual way and this can unsettle.

All that's on the down side. On the up side, many music videos display a tremendous exuberance and creativity: wonderfully imaginative, witty, humorous, inventive, entertaining, refreshing. They bring unique and often arresting visions of the world around us, encouraging the viewer to look at things in different ways. They are often playful, fun, as zesty as the music itself, and sometimes far better.

At their best, music videos are a celebration — of creativity, of vitality, of life itself in its many splendoured aspects: Billy Joel as a rough-bearded, hip ministering angel counselling a troubled teenager on the folly of suicide; Sting cavorting through a crazy crayon-cartoon landscape with schoolchildren singing about the seventh wave of universal love; Michael Jackson dancing like nobody else while cautioning against casual intimacy; Rod Stewart and Jeff Beck in a moving exhortation for one and all to get ready to ride the Lord's train to glory...and on and on.

While the huge production costs of videos have forced record companies to concentrate only on sure-fire money makers, they have had an opposite effect on the producers, allowing a new generation of talented unknowns a chance to practise their craft.

There is the hope that some of this creative magic will rub off on the video's big brother, the theatrical film. It could happen as soon as young directors cutting their teeth on

ROCK ON TRIAL

videos begin turning to the big screen (see for example U2's film *Rattle and Hum*). Certain aspects of music video have already rubbed off on the little screen in a big way; TV's 'Miami Vice,' for example, is clear, if not exactly encouraging, proof that others are eagerly watching the development of video.

Whether music video will become a mature art form in its own right or remain a clever promotional tool remains to be seen. Pressure has been brought to bear on producers of videos to clean up their acts and eradicate some of the more objectionable of the early excesses, a process which has already begun. In the meantime, we are treated to a front-row seat for a most fascinating show.

Stop, look, listen

So what are we to make of this phenomenon of rock video?

Like most other aspects of the music world (and the world at large for that matter), video offers both danger and opportunity.

The danger of videos is that the life of the inner person can be diminished, maybe even hardened or damaged by the rough, pernicious images fed to it. When the song's lyric, benign or otherwise, is married to a set of concrete images (often designed to push certain emotional or psychological buttons in the viewer/listener), the subjective, personal quality disappears and the protective or modifying role of the imagination is lost. The inner soul gets mugged.

The same danger exists with all television and films as well, and is by no means unique to rock videos.

Where there is danger, there is also opportunity. The opportunity for video is that a new art form can emerge which offers the possibility of enriching the lives of its consumers in new ways. The marriage of music to image is a potentially powerful instrument that can be employed in positive, life-enhancing ways.

▶ chapter 7
Too close for comfort
Rock and the gospel ▶

ROCK ON TRIAL

*O*ne of the constant struggles of a young rock group is finding a place to practise. I have practised with various bands in garages, basements, a condemned gymnasium, a converted root cellar and, once, even in a church. It is not every church that will let a rock group wail within its walls, but this particular church took an interest in us as musicians with a problem and helped out.

I was sitting alone in front of my amplifier one afternoon, practising riffs just before our practice session was to start when the minister's wife came into the room. She listened for a moment and walked over to me. 'You play beautifully,' she said.

This was embarrassing. 'Thanks,' I mumbled.

'You know, you really should think about using your talent for the Lord.' She was very serious. I didn't know what to say. She went on and told me how great it would be if I dedicated my music to serving God and reaching other young people for him. She has no idea what she's saying, I thought.

I listened politely, though I knew there was no way to do what she suggested, no practical way on earth. The reason was simple: the church would not accept the kind of music I played; it was too loud and raucous. She must have had in mind something softer, more traditional, only played with guitar and — well, why not? — maybe a drum, thus making it upbeat. She might have liked that kind of music, but nobody I knew would have listened to it.

At that time, contemporary Christian music was at an awkward stage, not satisfied with the traditional fare, but not yet ready to rock. Musicians who tried to push the limits using rock to put across the Christian message, ended up getting shut down or driven underground for their efforts.

But things were beginning to change; a new spirit was awakening people to the possibilities of joining the power of rock to the powerful message of Jesus Christ.

Mixing rock and religion

So far in this book we have been examining some of the controversies orbiting rock and pop music. My aim has not been to justify all the bad in rock, excuse it or explain away its faults. Instead, I have tried to offer some perspective on the problem, answer some of the major objections and show that there is nothing intrinsically wrong with rock as a style of music.

Once my friend Mike, from Mother Rush days, summed up the problem succinctly when he said, 'It's kind of like trying to defend a mode of transportation that's being exploited by bandits. There's nothing immoral about transportation, but the bandits have a way of corrupting everything they touch.' That is what has happened to rock, in a way. Bandits have all but ruined the vehicle of rock for a lot of people.

Yet, if rock is a wreck, I think it can be salvaged and even put to good use. J. G. Machen, in *Christianity and Culture*, suggests that 'the Christian cannot be satisfied as long as any human activity is either opposed to Christianity or out of all connection with Christianity... .The Christian, therefore, cannot be indifferent to any branch of human endeavour. It must be brought into some relationship with the gospel.'[1]

Many Christian musicians feel the same way. In fact a large number of them gather each year in the UK for the annual Greenbelt Festival. These musicians are committed to putting rock music to use for Christian entertainment, praise and worship, and for spreading the good news about Jesus Christ. Here is the cure for the nihilism and secular humanism afflicting popular music. Yet to rock's critics, the cure seems quite as bad as the disease. Rock and religion do not seem to mix.

▶ *Problem: Rock music is worldly music. As Christians we are called out of the world to live a spiritual life. When we imitate the world's music, we are directly disobeying the Bible's command to be separate from the world.*

Christians in all places and times have had trouble sorting out, let alone agreeing on, how much of this world is safe to participate in.

During the Middle Ages, groups of Christians formed independent communities, or monasteries, which were totally self-sufficient so that their members would not have to come into contact with a world they considered evil through and through. Others were not so fussy; declining complete separation, they merely adopted a different style of dress, an esoteric lingo, or different eating habits — anything that would help to remind them that they were not of the world.

Nowadays, most Christians dress pretty much like anybody else, and they do not live by themselves in walled cities, at least not in any great numbers. But various religious groups still make rules designed to keep worldly contact to an acceptable level. Every group seems to have laid down its own guidelines about fashions, customs, work, eating habits and any other aspect of living in the world. Music, since it is so much a part of the world, is often part of the proscription.

From the beginning, rock has been on the outs with organized religion. But when Christian musicians began picking up the rock style for use in Christian services and records, the 'Thou shalt not trespass' signs went up fast. The sound emanating from supposedly Christian records and radio stations were alarmingly similar to the sounds which the arbiters of Christian behaviour had fought so hard to keep at a far distance. It appeared that Christian music was contaminated by contact with worldly rock music. If rock is worldly, it can't be Christian...can it?

The answer to that question is clear in the minds of Christian musicians and those in decision-making positions within the Christian music industry. Whatever the larger Christian community thinks about linking the salvation message with worldly rock, Christian musicians themselves believe it's the only way to go.

From the days when only Cliff Richard was making the charts in Britain, Christian rock has won wider and wider acceptance — to the point where three of the top five gospel albums nominated for Grammy Awards in 1986 were rock. And when the darling of contemporary Christian music, Amy Grant, managed to land a song in America's Billboard Top Twenty, it was a snappy little rock tune, not a choir-backed hymn or inspirational favourite. Chicago's hard-rock Rez Band and the kinetic DeGarmo & Key band have both had music videos accepted and shown on America's MTV, while Britain's Greenbelt Festival is now part of the nation's rock calendar.

Undeniably, Christian rock is here to stay. 'And why not?' demand Christian musicians. 'If as Christians we are to be actively seeking the lost, sharing the good news, and calling them to Christ, what better way than in the very form that speaks to them best? We meet non-Christians where they are.'

Pharisees and weaker brothers

Reaching people with the Christian message through music is possible only if the music finds them. This means more, however, than just seeing that Christian records are placed in the hands of people who want to listen. It also means taking the message to people in a form they understand and relate to. That cannot happen as long as Christians maintain a fortress mentality — Us vs. Them.

Christians often fall into this trap. We retreat into ourselves because we fear becoming worldly. We erect a fortress around ourselves to keep the secular, or worldly, element from contaminating us. The world is approached as an enemy to be battled or retreated from. The main danger with this kind of thinking is that in keeping away from the world, we also remain isolated from the world's people who need the love, forgiveness and compassion only Christians can offer in the message of Jesus Christ.

True enough, the Bible does warn Christians on many occasions to keep free of worldly entanglements. But when the Bible speaks of worldliness, it is talking about falling into the world's sinful way of thinking, of allowing something else to take God's place in our lives. Worldliness is not mere contact with the world's people, places or things.

Jesus, in fact, explained that Christians were to remain in the world as an example to others. Jesus identified his enemy, and ours: the evil one. When he prayed for those who would come after him, Jesus said, 'My prayer is not that you take them out of the world but that you protect them from the evil one' (John 17:15). Salt preserves and protects; it seasons and has a good influence. Salt cannot do any good if it stays in the salt-cellar. It has to get sprinkled around.

When the apostle Paul warns, 'Do not conform any longer to the pattern of this world' (Romans 12:2), he is talking more about character than conduct. Restricting our participation in society is not his aim. He is more concerned about what kind of people we are than how we dress, what we eat, whether we have non-Christian friends or listen to rock music. An unnatural fear of becoming worldly or an obsessive preoccupation with working out what is or is not worldly is a telltale sign of the fortress mentality.

The fortress mentality is not a new problem; people in

TOO CLOSE FOR COMFORT

Jesus' day had trouble with it, too. Of all the groups Jesus came into contact with, two stand out in this regard: the Pharisees and, for lack of a better term, the weaker brothers.

The weaker brothers were those whose faith was fragile, who often stumbled and wavered in trying to carry out all that the Jewish law demanded. Although sincere, the weaker brothers were easily tempted and in constant need of repentance and reassurance. For them, religion was a struggle. Jesus had a great deal of sympathy for this group. He wanted to free them from the law's demands so they could establish personal contact with God.

The Pharisees were the superstars of Judaism. They knew the law forwards, backwards, and upside-down; they had faith to burn. Pharisees maintained a fanatical attention to detail, always weighing, judging and debating every action and consequence. In devotion and ambition, the Pharisees were second to none. They were the most pious people of the day, without question.

Yet, of all the people Jesus came in contact with, the Pharisees earned his harshest criticism. They made their religion a wall, with themselves on one side and everyone else on the other. They avoided contact with anyone who was not like them — which was everyone else. Their fastidiousness led them to condemn the lesser faith of others. Since no-one could outdo them, they placed themselves as the final authority on all religious matters, making themselves judges over all. The Pharisees reinforced the already burdensome Jewish law with hundreds of minute rules and regulations which mandated precise performances in every conceivable situation, thus further alienating their kinsmen from salvation. In time, as a result of their fortress mentality, the Pharisees developed a superiority complex: 'We're right and everyone else is wrong.'

Of course, the Pharisees did not see anything amiss in the way they lived. They thought of themselves as sincere, devoted Jews, doing only what God required. So thick had the walls grown that they no longer heard the cries from the other side. Ultimately, their fortress mentality led them to reject and murder God's own Son. This they did so their religion would not be corrupted by the 'worldly' ideas which Jesus taught. The Pharisees had become more spiritual than God.

We still have Pharisees and weaker brothers with us today. There are those who find rock music a stumbling block to their faith. Often these are new Christians whose old life is still painfully close. Rock may remind them of how they used to live. Like many new Christians, they want a dramatic outward change to go with their new inward change.

I have talked with people who have told me similar stories: 'When I first became a Christian I threw out all my rock albums. I couldn't bear to listen to them.' There is then a pause to reflect, and a rueful grin. 'Now, I just wish I had them back!'

It is not that the person is any less a Christian than before; on the contrary, he or she has become strong enough to enjoy the music once again without the negative associations. Of course, we should be careful of and sympathetic towards our weaker brothers, as Jesus was. Rock may not be for everyone; some, like recent converts, may need to give it up, at least until they achieve a degree of maturity and some distance from their old life. (I would advise anyone to give up anything that is keeping them from God.)

The apostle Paul speaks directly to this issue in the fourteenth and fifteenth chapters of Romans. In his day, however, the problem was not popular music but whether or not to drink wine, celebrate traditional holidays, or eat meat which had been offered to idols in pagan ceremonies. In essence, Paul's conclusion was that people have to decide questions of this nature for themselves, according to their own consciences and circumstances. Weaker brothers must be cared for. The strong must help them out.

Paul also has a few words to say to the weaker brothers: they are not to reproach those stronger than themselves, or find fault with their behaviour. This is important. Sometimes, I think, those who call themselves weaker brothers are really Pharisees. Outwardly, they may seem humble as they dutifully struggle through life. But inwardly they nurture great pride in their abstinence from things they consider worldly. Worse, they try to impose the same restrictions on others on the grounds that, 'Remember the weaker brother; you shouldn't cause him to stumble.' Of course, the weaker brother is imaginary: they have no actual person in mind at all. The Pharisee is only using the idea of a weaker brother to force compliance with his petty rules. We should recognize that deception for what it is.

Jesus' criticism of the Pharisees and his compassion for the weaker brothers offers a way of dealing with the problem of worldliness and rock music. The difference between Jesus' and the Pharisees' style of reaching people is plain. Jesus did not mind being seen with ordinary people. He went wherever he had to go to be heard, even to the homes of thieves and worse — places no self-respecting Pharisees would be seen dead in. It was the religious leaders who would have nothing to do with sinners. Jesus knew he had nothing to fear from the world; it held no seductive power over him. He was free to take his message anywhere, using any form of communication available for his purpose. Besides, he actually enjoyed talking to Gentiles, visiting tax collectors, conversing with women, attending feasts, turning water into wine — activities which scandalized the pious of his day. His attitude of involvement, of breathing deep of life, is our example.

Rock music has the ability to reach many people where they live. Coupled with the Christian message it becomes a very powerful form of communication — much more powerful than many traditional forms since some people turn off such approaches. Being powerful doesn't make it worldly.

Christian musicians have found the rock form to be a useful and exciting tool to spread the Christian message.

ROCK ON TRIAL

They like rock music themselves, of course. It resonates with them, and so it's only natural that they use it to communicate to their audiences what is most precious to them.

Those not comfortable with it must be careful in condemning it. The Bible offers a parallel. Jesus' disciples, filled with the Holy Spirit, picked up teaching and healing people where Jesus left off. The Jewish leaders, thinking they had put an end to that sort of nonsense by crucifying Jesus, called a special meeting to decide what to do with his troublesome followers. The council was all for killing the disciples, too, when one of their wiser members took the floor. Gamaliel reminded the council of a few similar cases and then said, 'Leave these men alone! Let them go! For if their purpose or activity is of human origin, it will fail. But if it is of God, you will not be able to stop these men; you will only find yourselves fighting against God' (Acts 5:38-39).

chapter 8
Give me that old time religion
Rock and its critics

ROCK ON TRIAL

Rock, as we saw in chapter four, did not come exclusively from Africa but developed out of many cultural influences in America. Black America's role in forming new kinds of music has been well documented by others. When the lines are drawn, they suggest an interesting conclusion: rock originated out of Christian music.

Richard Stanislaw, music columnist and professor of music at an American college, backs up this assertion. 'Rock,' he says, 'has a special claim to the attention of believers because of its history. Rock was first Christian music, then appropriated by the popular secular culture. Decades before Top 40 radio stations discovered rhythm and blues, the style was almost exclusively used for "gospel!" '[1]

Still, many Christians cannot accept the idea of taking rock back to its original purpose. They cannot see how any kind of music with such powerful rhythms, which exerts such a force on our physical senses, can be used for God.

▶ *Problem: Rock is basically a 'body' music appealing to people on a sensual level. The driving sound and rhythm seduces the listeners, urging them to indulge in physical pleasures. How can such music communicate anything spiritual?*

Rock is a simple, straightforward style of music; listeners

can easily apprehend the beat and follow along, tap their feet or clap their hands or bob their heads or whatever. A march can have a similar effect — it encourages our feet to move. That's great! People should feel free to participate physically when they are moved by music. Many of us have lost our ability to move spontaneously in time to music — our inhibitions or perhaps our theology has atrophied this innate capacity to move, something that children do naturally and unself-consciously.

Notice that music doesn't *make* people clap their hands or stomp their feet or move their bodies or march down the street. It's just easier and more fun to do it with the music than without.

Other kinds of music are more intellectual in their approach. Much of classical music might be called 'head music' since it is complex and intellectual. Appreciation of classical music may take a little training, but it has never been satisfactorily explained to me why head music is better or more spiritual than body music. Is rock music wrong because it is easy to feel? Is there something sinful about physical feelings?

My theology tells me that God created and is interested in every aspect of me — the physical, emotional, mental and spiritual person that I am. I may meet God mind to mind, as many people seem to think is best. More often I meet him when I am working (physical), or in the midst of an enjoyable or an anxious experience (emotional). Or I meet him when I least expect it, when something moves within and my spirit tells me he is near (spiritual). In other words, my relationship with God involves my total self. Why, then, should one kind of music be considered more appropriate for relating to God than another?

Straight from the heart

In the Middle Ages, various groups of people 'denied the flesh' for God. They starved themselves, dressed in rags, refused to bathe or comb their hair, and when that was not enough, flogged themselves senseless with whips. The idea was that all this denying made them more spiritual since they were no longer given over to the gross desires of the body. Their asceticism, however, did not necessarily make them more spiritual. But it did make them hungry, dirty, smelly, ragged and sore.

While the idea of whipping the body to prove spirituality is not in vogue today, people still believe that the body is the inferior member of the body-spirit partnership, and a major stumbling block on the road to heaven. In certain instances, perhaps it is; but it is also our only vehicle for carrying out God's will. God created the whole body; he created it wholly good, not the seat of sin unimaginable.

The accusation that rock is body music centres on the idea that the beat arouses sexual impulses. The implication is that the beat starts and suddenly the frail human organism is assaulted by an erotic flood tide of powerful physical urges too overwhelming to deny. A lot of people harbour suspicions of this sort, apparently forgetting that sex is not like sneezing.

In other words, sex is one physical activity which derives from the complex interplay of mental and emotional factors, many of which are only dimly understood. At any rate, the human sexual response is a *learned* response. It is not instinctual, and is not triggered by the presence of certain chemicals or hormones racing pell-mell through the bloodstream — which would seem to have more to do with the phases of the moon or some other biological rhythm, rather than that a certain style of music wafts out over the airwaves.

If people get sexually excited listening to rock music, it is because they have learned to do so. Since it is a learned response, it can be consciously controlled, as can any other aspect of behaviour.

Obviously, a man might get excited watching a voluptuous woman wriggle around to a rock beat. I would maintain, however, that this has less to do with the style of music being played than with the visual drama being displayed.

Having sexual feelings is not sinful. Even acting on sexual feelings is not wrong, provided it is within the framework prescribed by the Bible.

I believe the apostle Paul spoke to this idea when he said, 'To the pure, all things are pure' (Titus 1:15). Notice he did not say, 'To the pure some things are pure' or 'most things are pure.' He said *all* things, extending the boundaries quite far indeed, opening the door for a more liberated approach once the biblical foundation has been laid. For if our attitudes and intentions are pure, how can the object of our desire be otherwise? Furthermore, those fleshly desires we worry so much about would not be a problem if our hearts were right, because a right heart moderates all of the body's actions. We have nothing to fear from sex, food, games, drink, music or whatever, if our hearts are pure in God's sight.

'For a Christian musician, it takes a measure of maturity to use rock music with responsibility,' notes veteran Christian musician Chuck Girard. 'But when it's used with the right attitude, the sensual nature of rock is vastly diminished — it becomes a spiritual music.'

Naturally, the same could be said for any other kind of music, since what we are dealing with here is the very nature of music itself.

They're playing my song

Music is quite possibly pure communication, since in many ways it seems to bypass the intellect and speak directly to the inner person. This communication is of such a special quality that for thousands of years people have considered music to be somewhat mystical or even supernatural. Music is not supernatural, but it is certainly mysterious in the way it involves us.

Music is therefore, primarily, nonverbal communication — pure expression. Even when accompanied by a meaningful lyric, it is the wordless side of music which gives it special effect. If the same meanings and emotions could be as easily expressed in words, there probably would be no need for music. Music is able to impart special meaning to a smile, a longing, the touch of a friend, a kiss. The best verbal attempts often fall miles short of the mark.

Be that as it may, the old saw 'music is the universal language' is only half true. Music may be universal, but it is a language only to those who can understand its various dialects. Just as each separate culture creates its own unique modes of expression (styles of dress, language, customs), so it cultivates its own musical forms. Music takes on the peculiar ability to communicate to the culture that produces it; outsiders will likely be baffled and confused. This much can be readily observed: the music of one culture will often be totally meaningless to the members of another culture. For example, the music of certain mountain tribes in China seems eerie and otherworldly, to Western ears unintelligible. Yet it carries deep significance to those who understand it.

Music as nonverbal communication creates a sense of belonging for those who understand it. It is a primary function of music to provide this feeling of belonging. Rock music is extremely effective in speaking to its particular tribe — young people — and in providing them with a feeling of belonging. Here is where the intent of the music comes into play.

The intent of a song has to do with the type of message the songwriter puts into the song, in the lyrics as well as the instrumental notes. The songwriter's intention may not be all that easy to ascertain merely by looking at the words; but when a well-made song is played, there is usually no mistake what the songwriter was communicating. Thus, even when the intent is not easily expressed verbally, the emotional impact of the song is usually unmistakable. The message comes through loud and clear emotionally, whether or not it is grasped cognitively.

Every churchgoer has had an experience with music's

ability to telegraph meaning directly to the heart. As the typical Sunday morning service begins, worshippers file in and take their seats while an organ prelude calms and quiets, creating a peaceful atmosphere, turning the hearts of the congregation toward worship. At the end of the service, the reverberating, forceful chords of the postlude dismiss the worshippers, challenging them to a week of renewed strength and faith. No-one misses the message although no words were sung. It is implicit.

When the rhythms of rock are put to use with the intention of worship, praise, edification or any other higher purpose, it becomes a distinctly different animal from the raging, devouring beast roaming at large through many rock albums. It is different because it is infused with a different intent and purpose. The higher purpose of Christian rock is clearly telegraphed to the hearts of listeners. Stripped of its drugs-and-booze disposition, its overt sexual connotations, its pandering exploitation, and then recharged with positive energy, Christian rock stands far apart from the secular variety. This much can be easily demonstrated.

Look at the audience of most Christian concerts: well-behaved, attentive, appreciative, excited, considerate, worshipful even — although the style of music may be virtually the same as that which stirs up the masses at a Rolling Stones' concert. Quite clearly, people respond to the intent of the music, and to all the attendant stimuli, not just rhythm or beat as is so often supposed.

The devil's due

Still, many conscientious Christians believe that rock is intrinsically evil, a thing spawned by the devil to entrap unwary humans, to seduce them and lead them to ruin. Hence, anything which the devil has devised cannot contain any spiritual potential. The very form corrupts what it touches; any enterprise which attempts to use it is doomed from the beginning.

Those who promote such a view are making two serious

mistakes simultaneously: overestimating the devil's power and underestimating his subtlety.

Satan is not all-powerful; he does not possess the ability to create anything. He can only use whatever we give him; in that, however, he is virtually unlimited. Apparently, there is no end to what he can get from people to use against them. He is well schooled in the weaknesses of the human frame; he knows what we are, and where we are the most vulnerable. And he will meet us there, at the point of our greatest weakness.

If one is prone to ego trips, Satan is there. If sex is the weak point, he will use that. If money is where the heart is, or power or fame or ambition, Satan will employ that to destroy. If a young person is easily led by the crowd, Satan knows it, and he will use it for his own end if allowed. He can use religion. One of his favourite ruses is to allow the security of empty ritual and blind, misguided emotionalism (which distorts true faith and even kills it) to replace true spirituality. Thus the victims of this trap never perceive their demise, so secure are they in the knowledge that they are very religious and, therefore, very safe.

The devil does not care what he uses to undermine the truth. We flatter him in thinking that he creates special traps or holds sway in a province of his own design. Those who treat rock music as the devil's domain have forgotten that Satan is the father of lies, and chaos is his calling. He can create nothing, only pervert the good things God has created, bending them to his own ends.

An error is made, too, in thinking that what the devil uses cannot be redeemed. Music is the gift of the all-powerful, eternally loving God who continually redeems his creation. Nothing is beyond his restoring power or ever far from his grace. Thus music, in whatever form, is God's. It need not have an overt spiritual emphasis to be spiritual or to speak to us in a meaningful way. To call something which God has made 'satanic' at once magnifies Satan's limited power and diminishes God's supreme authority.

▶ chapter 9
Sacred cows and Trojan horses

Rock and evangelism ▶

ROCK ON TRIAL

I have seen strange things in church: karate demonstrations, magic shows, chalk talks, singing saws, trained birds, puppets, ventriloquists and more. I have read of preachers practising all sorts of weirdness to catch the attention of their congregations. One promised fishburgers for every member of the congregation if they could round up 5,000 people for a morning service. The undisputed champion is the minister who doused himself with lighter fluid and set fire to his clothing as he stood in his pulpit, demonstrating to his horrified congregation what he thought the flames of hell would be like. I even heard of a converted stripper who did her 'striptease for God,' hoping to lure in the unwary and then shock them with the gospel.

The point is, of course, to attract attention, you have to draw a crowd. And once you have the curious onlookers hooked, you can slip in a little good news.

To many, the approach lacks honesty; it smacks of the con game. Show business and Christianity shouldn't mix; when they do, it causes difficulties. One or the other is co-opted by the performance and the cry of 'Compromise!' goes up.

▶ *Problem: Rock is a Trojan horse trotted out to trick nonbelievers into accepting Christ. People are drawn to the glitter and glamour and not the Lord. The gospel is compromised and cheapened by such deception and by association with the self-serving, commercial nature of show business.*

Boiled down, this problem is one of communication: how far are Christians allowed to go to reach unbelievers? Throughout history Christians have pounced on every new advance in the field of communication to spread the good news. When Johann Gutenberg came up with his notion of movable type, it was for printing the Bible, not one mother's favourite dumpling recipe. Religious pamphlets, magazines and books of all kinds have poured off the presses ever since. With the advent of radio and television, the public airwaves were soon abuzz with scores of radio and television evangelists. The sermons and musings of some American evangelists are bounced off satellites to the far corners of the earth. Some Bible teachers now record their studies and lectures on film and video so that they can reach a wider audience.

Oddly, the art of Christian communication has not always kept pace with the hardware and technical expertise. Too often we have used brand new methods to preach in a dated, outmoded style. So, for all our space-age gear, we can end up talking not to the lost who need to hear, but only to other Christians already front-row centre for the performance. Paul Johnson, a Christian musician and composer, put it well:

> Today the church faces a world that is not the least bit interested in hearing us defend our sacred cows. It is interested, however, in hearing the solution to the crises it faces in the realm of personal identity, economy, ecology, ethics, guilt, hope for the world's future...all of which have profound solutions in the person of Jesus Christ.
>
> As a Christian musician, I find these crises and solutions worthy of musical composition. Indeed, I have discovered that music is one of the most profound methods of communicating what I believe on these issues.

> I do find, however, that the limitations and restrictions which Christians have placed on sacred music in the past make my task as a Christian musician in today's world difficult.
>
> If I must limit my method of communication to robed choirs and a pipe organ to retain a sacred label for my work as a communicator of the gospel, then my job is defeated before it begins.[1]

Johnson is not the only contemporary musician who has felt the frustration of trying to fit the everlasting message to an updated style within the church's narrowly defined limits of acceptability. It is not merely a problem of keeping up with the times; there is a basic misunderstanding of how rock music communicates.

To some traditionalists, the message of rock is drowned out in the din of screaming guitars and the crashing rhythms of the drums. They feel that rock, as a low form of music, is not fit to clothe the heavenly gospel. Thus anything communicated by the flashy style will be cheapened in the process.

Rock musicians, on the other hand, feel that to those familiar with the language of rock it has a power to speak where other means fail. There is nothing cheap about that. They see rock as a legitimate way to meet non-Christians on their own territory, to earn the right to be heard by speaking a common language and speaking it with integrity.

Anyone with a sense of history will recognize that this is not an original scheme, but one that has been continually used in the church through the ages.

New wine into old wineskins

Composers of church music in all eras have struggled to equip their faith with suitable new music. For the most part it has been a struggle against sentimentality. Christians by and large have a maddening habit of firmly planting themselves at any point where pleasant feelings have touched their faith. They say, 'This is good; let's keep it

SACRED COWS AND TROJAN HORSES

this way.' That was Peter's mistake at the transfiguration.

Jesus had taken his three closest disciples up on the mountain with him to witness at first hand his glory undiminished. The disciples saw Moses; they saw Elijah; they saw Christ transfigured, and they heard the voice of God. Peter was especially impressed, and fell on his face, crying, 'This is wonderful! Let's make three tents, one for you, one for Moses and one for Elijah.' He wanted to preserve the moment forever, forgetting that the life Jesus requires is not static but active, not resting on past pleasures or achievements but moving ahead.

Several years ago, the music director of the church I was attending closed the service with the congregation singing an old favourite, Luther's 'A mighty fortress' — only an upbeat version, heavily syncopated. The congregation, myself included, gamely struggled through the new arrangement, not once but twice, to get the hang of it. After the service I heard many members comment that the new version was interesting, but they preferred the 'original.' I agreed. In fact, there was a bit of grumbling to that effect until the ignorant among us were informed that we had, indeed, sung the original arrangement. We had sung it the way Luther had written it! Most were upset because it was simply different from the version we usually sing.

Look in any hymnal at the dates of the hymns the church is singing: 1742, 1611, 1535, 1409. The dates reach back and back, through the Middle Ages and into the first few centuries of the early church. Of course, the main bulk of our hymns date from the 1800s, deriving from the great revivals of the last century. And while there may be a few from the first decades of the current century, most of the hymns we sing in our churches are hymns with a long and glorious past. We 'moderns' with our almost unlimited access to the past are worse hoarders than our ancestors. The relatively recent capability of instantaneous global communication, and the distribution of knowledge and scholarship that it generates, allows us to store and keep, not only the work of the masters, but the work of the not-so-great as well. In the arena of church music, this means we end up revering some music as sacred and everlasting which was only meant to have a brief life, music which was to speak to a particular time and then give way to something else.

M. Goldbeck, noted music historian, made the observation that until the end of the nineteenth century, music gravitated around the present. The music of the day was always *contemporary*. Churchgoers in Bach's day heard Bach's *latest* composition, for example.[2] Today, church music orbits the past, circling around the whole history and tradition of music.

In this, modern Christians have tricked themselves into thinking that contemporary sounds are somehow less worthy of carrying the Christian message. Yet such a notion never occurred to churchgoers of even two hundred years ago.

Martin Luther wrote hymns for his reformation effort, giving music back to the common people. Charles Wesley did the same, using drinking songs and fitting them with meaningful Christian lyrics. Others followed and eventually the idea of using common forms of communication to speak to Christians and non-Christians alike became an approved and established practice. Apparently, this practice was lost somewhere along the way, at least where music is concerned.

It is time to bring back the idea of taking a normal, commonly recognized vehicle — like rock — and putting it into Christian service. Rock musicians are convinced that traditional church music has little effect on a non-Christian world and virtually none on the rock generation. Singing about 'bringing in the sheaves' or 'marching to Zion' communicates nothing to those who do not know what sheaves are or where in the world Zion might be. In fact, some of our sacred songs do not have much, beyond sentimentality, to recommend them to most Christians either.

Even the most familiar hymns of the church are often sung

by rote without any real understanding. Every Sunday millions of Christians unwittingly make statements in hymns that they would be embarrassed or unwilling to make otherwise. 'Take my silver and my gold, not a mite would I withhold... .' Nice sentiment, but certainly not something you actually see happen in real life. Sometimes the hymns themselves defy common-sense understanding, as in, 'That with the world, myself, and thee, I, ere I sleep, at peace, may be,' or, 'Here I raise mine Ebenezer.' What is mine Ebenezer? You must be sharp indeed to unravel the meaning of these phrases, or the host of others like them, which populate church hymnals. Yet who gives them a second thought?

In *Protestant Worship Music*, Charles Etherington makes the observation that part of the unreality which traditional church music often has for modern ears lies in the fact that so much of it reflects thoughts and feelings of the past.

> Certainly the music cannot mean very much if it is a medium through which people express thoughts that have no meaning for them... Although contemporary music is often considered merely for entertainment value, a person will often come closer to a realization of God's presence through hearing serious music at home or in the concert hall than he does in church. This statement may seem incredible and even shocking to people who are not musically sensitive, but a moment's reflection should persuade them that there is nothing strange in the thought of God making himself felt through any medium that will awaken a response.[3]

Watch your language!

The charge that rock is a Trojan horse used to trick non-believers into becoming Christians is based on a narrow notion of what evangelism means.

Larry Norman tells the tale of a Christian who is out on the street witnessing. Along comes a non-believer who inadvertently wanders into range.

'Have you heard the good news?'

'No, what is it?' the non-believer asks enthusiastically.

'You're going to hell!' the Christian bellows.

The bewildered non-Christian scratches his head, plucks up his courage and asks, 'Uh...What's the *bad* news?'

We frequently make one of two mistakes when we set out to talk to non-Christians. Either we address ourselves to other Christians and hope non-Christians are listening somewhere close by and somehow get the message, or we plunge headlong into an invasion of non-Christian territory, guns blazing. Both approaches are ill-founded, because they make non-Christians run for cover.

In the United States of America (and increasingly in other countries via satellite) often the most irrelevant language is used by certain TV evangelists. Thunder-throated preachers boom out the salvation plan for one and all, telling non-Christians how evil, mean, wicked, bad and nasty they really are — but we love you, brother, we really do — and using such telltale phrases as 'lost in sin,' 'everlasting fire,' 'washed in the blood of the lamb,' 'throne of redemption,' 'saved by grace,' and so on.

Now, if you had a message to give to the Chinese, would you insist that the entire Chinese mainland first learn English before you delivered the message? No, you would find a way to translate your message so they could understand it.

To many non-Christians, Christianity is a foreign language which they do not comprehend. Yet we think if we just keep talking at them, they will somehow get the message. So we preach and preach and preach. Our actions preach, and our music preaches — all in this obscure, somewhat frightening foreign language. It can be rare indeed to find a Christian who is willing to learn the non-Christian's language before attempting to share the gospel. But the basic principle of evangelism should be communication, and communicating the good news involves identifying with people, speaking their language.

Rock communicates to the rock generation. It has the ability to reach a population that has grown up with it. Young people identify with it readily, much more so than with, for example, some elaborate 'God slot' television pageant which may give Christians comfort, but does very little for the nonbelievers.

Our Christian message can be carried effectively through rock music. Those who say that this somehow compromises the gospel are forgetting one thing: communication *is* compromise. You talk; I listen. Then I talk and you listen. Without this basic agreement, based on a mutual give-and-take, nothing happens. Both parties must be free and open to the other; speakers must speak to listeners in ways they can understand — otherwise, speech is meaningless.

Just because I speak in a way you can understand does not mean that I have watered down the content of my message, only that I am willing to meet you where you are.

Christian crossover

Compromise of another sort is very much a live issue for many Christian musicians, who, with the growing acceptance of Christian rock, have become acutely aware of the special pitfalls created by success. As Christian rock has grown in favour, the temptations to sell out have increased proportionately.

Only a few years ago record sales of ten or fifteen thousand copies were considered admirable for a Christian rock band. Today worldwide sales in excess of one hundred thousand and more per album are not at all uncommon. A few Christian artists have gold, even platinum records hanging on their walls. Of course, the Christian audience for Christian music has expanded dramatically, but Christian artists have also worked very hard to take their music and their message to the larger non-Christian world as well — a process known as 'crossover' — that is, an artist (or group) who breaks out of the normal classification and crosses category boundaries.

A country-western singer is said to have a hit record when it tops the specialist country-western charts; she has a crossover when her record tops the country-western charts and 'crosses over' onto the pop charts as well. Crossover always helps an artist because it has the effect of enlarging the artist's audience.

This is precisely what some Christian artists have achieved, and what many more are working toward — having their music (and its message) cross over into the larger pop category. Because contemporary Christian music — like country-western, soul, jazz and classical — is a relatively small market when compared to pop, and because reaching people with the message of the gospel is the name of the game, it only makes sense to try to reach as many as possible. Crossover increases the audience, and more people are reached.

But when the audience increases, career considerations become more complicated. Options multiply, doors open, opportunities come knocking. Money flows more freely.

The relative success of Christian music over the last few years has many Christian artists thinking long and hard about their motives and motivations. And many are walking the tightrope between commercial success and compromise more carefully than ever.

Naturally, compromise is an issue for any Christian engaged in a career, not musicians alone. But people who stand in the spotlight are more easily and more carefully scrutinized. And because they are so visible, their lives and motivations have to be above reproach — more so than other, less visible Christians, because what a performer says and does is witnessed by so many more people.

Virtually everything a Christian performer does is called into question. Amy Grant succeeds in getting a song on the American Billboard Top 20, and her tune receives airplay around the world — yet, her fellow Christians fret, 'Why isn't there more about Jesus in that song?'

The heavy metal band, Stryper, dress in black-and-yellow

spandex tights laced with chains and record their ear-smashing music on a secular record label. Christians grumble, 'If they're really Christians, why do they dress like that?'

Actually, these bewildered Christians (we'll give them the benefit of the doubt and assume that they aren't Pharisees in disguise) only want to be reassured that the performers have not sold out their faith for the bright lights and easy money of success.

Certainly excesses have been committed and mistakes made in this area. In the battle for acceptance and legitimacy there have been a few casualties. Success will bring more. And because this tricky war is waged in such a hostile arena with such a volatile weapon, we should not be aghast or outraged when one of our soldiers falls. Rather, we should be there on the front lines with them, praying, supporting, helping and binding wounds when necessary.

Mr. Booth's brass band

Christian rock musicians only seek to do in today's world what William Booth, founder of the Salvation Army, did with his brass bands toward the end of the last century. Brass bands, you must understand, did not meet with the full approval of the religious-minded of that day. Booth's small touring groups were subject to heckling and embarrassment. Their meetings were broken up on occasion by drivers herding horses and buggies through the scattering streetside throng. But the idea survived to become an institution of its own.

At Christmas 1879, Booth wrote, 'Every note, and every strain, and every harmony is divine and belongs to us.' And he ordered Christians to 'bring out your cornets and harps and organs and flutes and violins and pianos and drums, and everything else that can make a melody. Offer them to God, and use them to make all the hearts about you merry before the Lord.'[4]

To the average person on the street today, the words 'Salvation Army Band' conjure up a quaint image of a bygone era. But the idea behind it is still a good one: take the message to the people who need to hear it in a way they can understand and respond to it.

I am not suggesting that we do away with everything that has gone before, only that we should make room for Christian rock artists to take their place among all the others who have given meaningful expression to our faith. For there are many among us who desperately seek what we all need: a music which expresses rather than alienates itself from our deepest convictions, which does not pander to us but ennobles us by its self-conscious dedication to the glory of God.

▶ chapter 10

You gotta have art

Rock and the standards of art ▶

Ever see anybody try to row a boat with one oar? Or a sailboat traverse a lake without a rudder? It's next to impossible. No sailor would willingly put to sea in a boat without oars or a rudder. To do so would be foolish, possibly disastrous.

Yet, every day, thousands of people embark on the voyage of a lifetime with neither oars nor rudder — nor compass. They are young people who come of age and begin thinking for themselves; most have not been given the proper equipment for making the right decisions, for steering themselves through life.

I always remember my friend Gary. Gary grew up in a family that did not believe in going to films. Sometimes there would be a film my parents would allow me to see, and I would invite Gary. But the answer was always the same: no films. Later, as we grew older and entered high school, Gary was left to make those kinds of decisions on his own. Consequently, he started going to every film that came to town. It didn't matter what the picture was, Gary would watch it. The best and the absolute worst alike, Gary watched them all.

I went with him to a double feature once. After the first film, I asked him, 'How did you like it?'

'Great,' he said. When the second was over he said, 'Man, that was great too.'

YOU GOTTA HAVE ART

'What are you saying?' I asked, shocked. 'That movie was horrible! Awful! A total waste of time!'

'Oh,' was all he said. He couldn't tell the difference: all he knew was that he liked films. As elementary as it seems, no-one had ever given him a hint as to how he might tell the good ones from the bad ones, how to choose which ones to watch and which to stay away from. To him they were all the same.

Those who condemn all of rock have nurtured thousands of Garys, people who can't tell good music from bad because they have no guidelines for judging it.

In this way, those so violently opposed to rock have done a great disservice to young people. Because of their total condemnation ('Rock is wrong; don't listen to any of it') they have left thousands of people with no way to judge effectively a large part of contemporary culture. And without guidelines, it's easy to drift into confusion and error. Sooner or later people must be allowed to think and choose for themselves how they will live. It would be far better to provide a good foundation and training in making the right decisions before that time comes.

A good foundation consists of knowing what is good and what is bad, and the ability to tell them apart. When you know what is good and how to recognize it, the choice is easy. However, when it comes to art (and when we talk about music we are talking about art), most people do not know what makes good art good, or how to recognize it.

Art does not come affixed with a prepasted label which neatly lumps it into one of two categories: classic or garbage. Everything of artistic endeavour exists on a continuum, a wide spectrum spanning all that is superior or good at one end, and that which is inferior or bad at the other.

Music, like painting, theatre, literature, sculpture, pottery, dance and all the rest of art, must exhibit that vital spark which allows it to transcend the mere mechanics of its creation if it is to be judged superior. Good music, in whatever style, must possess all the qualities we have come to expect of good art: uniqueness, craftsmanship, maturity, intelligence, wholeness and spontaneity.

Clearly, an entire style of music cannot labelled good or bad; only individual pieces of music can be judged. The better we understand the qualities of the good, the better able we will be to tell the good from the bad in rock music, or any other kind of music or art. Here are some qualities of good art.

Uniqueness. This is the attribute or originality, of never having been before. A work bearing this trait will seem new and novel, and to a certain extent, inventive. It says, 'I am one of a kind.'

Craftsmanship. This is the technical aspect of the work, how well it is made. Whether referring to a sculpture or a song, the skill of the maker will be apparent. Good art reflects a high degree of skill. Also, the skill must be appropriate to the medium. For example, a sculptor and a potter may both work in clay, but they will do very different things with it. Their skills are not the same. You cannot say to the potter, 'You are a poor craftsman because you can't make a lifelike statue,' or say to the sculptor, 'You lack the proper skills because your work is not functional.' Those statements are nonsense because potters and sculptors are working in different mediums, even if they are working with the same materials. It is the same with music. Whether a rock song or a symphony, the work should say, 'I was made by an expert.'

Maturity. When you think of something being mature, you think of it being fully developed. A work which fails to reach its full potential and remains at an elementary level can be said to be infantile, lacking in maturity. This does not mean there is no place for the simple, the basic, the profound. Often the highest expression of maturity is found in the studied application of the most basic elements. A mature work will say, 'I am full-grown.'

Intelligence. In order for any piece of art to be considered good, it must be understandable. It must be a work of

YOU GOTTA HAVE ART

reason; that it, it must show us something of the mind of its creator. An intelligent work will show a degree of imagination, cleverness and perhaps wit. Rather than presenting a jumble of half-formed ideas, good art shows the work of the mind in selecting, assembling and developing its raw materials. It must reveal intelligence in design and require reason and logic to fully apprehend its beauty. Art with intelligence says, 'I am refined.'

Wholeness. As with a good story, a good song must satisfy the listener; there can be no loose ends and no missing pieces. Wholeness means that a particular work has made full use of its opportunities and that it stands alone as a finished entity. In a sense, a work demonstrating wholeness fulfils our expectations, delivering all it promises. It is not fragmented or made from separate parts patched together. Its parts have been totally unified. A work with the quality of wholeness says, 'I am complete.'

Spontaneity. In art, spontaneity does not mean that a work suddenly springs into existence full-blown. However, many works of art appear as if they *were* instantaneously created. They have a lively, animated appearance, capable of engaging their audience. An artist may have slaved for years over a work, pouring out his or her soul upon it, but the piece must never appear forced or stale or work worn. Spontaneity also suggests that the work has a life of its own, apart from the artist. It sometimes appears that the work has always existed. The great Michelangelo once made a comment to the effect that the subjects of his sculptures already lived within the mighty blocks of marble; he only carved away the stone to set them free. A work with spontaneity says, 'I am alive.'

For most of the rock audience, and even the most discriminating critics, it would be enough to be be given good art. But for Christians, that is not enough; we must also be concerned with the art's *message*.

The four arts

In his book, *Art and the Bible*, Francis Schaeffer described four categories of art: bad art with a true message; good art with a true message; bad art with a false message; and good art with a false message.[1] These are what I call the four arts, and they all abound in the soup of the contemporary music scene. Good and bad art with their respective messages exist side by side and back to back in the music world. Listen to any Top 40 radio station; you will hear from ten to fifteen different songs in an hour, each with a different message.

Christians, desiring truth in all areas of life, require true messages in music as well. Sorting out true messages from false ones is not particularly difficult, but when music is added to give impetus to the message, it tends to confuse things. The distinctions blur; grey areas appear. If the music is catchy and the lyrics pleasing, listeners could find themselves accepting a message they might otherwise reject.

In this regard, one of the four arts is quite treacherous. Bad art with a true message is not likely to make much of an impact; the message, despite its worth, is buried under the inferiority of the music. The same could be said for bad art with a false message. People seldom take bad art seriously; whatever message accompanies it is not taken seriously either.

Good art operates in reverse of that principle. Good art with a true message is held in high esteem; the message is reinforced by the quality of the art. This is the best, but danger lies close by. When good art is coupled with a false message, the message gains importance. It takes on a credibility it would not, could not and should not ordinarily have. In responding to the goodness of the art, people may suspend judgement and accept the false message, too.

I do not mean to suggest, as some do, that rock performers actually *try* to trick people into believing something that is false; it just happens. In the clash between the images and

YOU GOTTA HAVE ART

illusions of the rock world, rock singers are likely to say things in public and in song which are not necessarily true — for any number of reasons.

As often as not, musicians are themselves ignorant of the truth and consequently in no position to communicate the truth to others. What they say may be part of their public image; it is demanded by their created persona and has no direct bearing on reality. Or else they simply speak to a commonly assumed reality, such as 'love makes the world go round,' 'you only live once; so grab for the gusto,' 'as long as you're happy, nothing else matters,' and the like. These are nothing more than the myths of the modern world. Rock singers do not have to believe these myths to sing songs about them; many performers assume that these sentiments are what their audiences want to hear, or what will make a record sell. Time and again rock musicians come back to certain stock themes for their songs, themes which are almost universally accepted.

Generally speaking, when it comes to communicating true messages, rock falls down in the following areas:

Materialism. Although many songwriters point out that wealth and material things can never ensure happiness, a good many more imply just the opposite. When Madonna bellows out that she's a material girl living in a material world, her tongue isn't completely in her cheek. Success is often presented stereotypically: obtaining more, getting your share, making your fortune, having it all, and so on. Christians know this philosophy to be false.

Sex. Love in rock is usually physical love. Both men and women are presented as sexual objects existing solely to satisfy the desires of the other. Relationships in songs often focus on the sex act as the ultimate expression of love. This is only an imitation of love, of course. Christians recognize many other dimensions of the word *love* which are rarely portrayed in song. Yet rock is too often content to mirror the immature aspects of sexual love, rather than explore the subject on a deeper, more mature level.

Hedonism. The good life is a part of the rock myth. Self-indulgence is a personal right. Personal pleasure is the highest aim in life; there is no point in denying anything that helps you obtain pleasure. The Christian value of service is foreign to most popular songs.

There are undoubtedly several other theme areas which could be identified, but these suffice for the bulk of popular music. Not all songs have clearly defined themes; their messages may be mixed, containing elements of several different themes. Some songs are subtle in their approach, others more obvious. U2 is a good example of a group that is oriented to the secular market but whose songs are filled with Christian allusions. Some songs present messages that leap into active conflict with Christian values, and others present true messages — though they may not be written or performed with a distinctly Christian point of view. The song 'People Get Ready' is one recent and noteworthy example, recorded by none other than Rod 'Tartan Terror' Steward and Jeff Beck, whose speciality is screaming guitars. Yet, these two turned in a plaintive, even heart-rending performance of this old gospel tune that warns of the danger of sin and the rewards of salvation through Christ. What is more, they did it with class.

Use it or lose it

So, in the tangle of mixed messages presented by popular music, it is left to the listener to decide what is true and what is false in a song, to embrace the truth and reject the lie. I believe all Christians are called to be discriminating listeners, not only of rock music but of everything they hear. If we appreciate the privilege of listening to rock music — both Christian rock and the music of the secular culture — we must seize the responsibility of thinking about what is being listened to and weeding out the good from the bad by applying the standards of good art and by examining the message.

Everyone must become a critic — weighing the difference

between what is acceptable and what is unacceptable in rock music — or forfeit the right to choose. There are plenty of people who are eager to dictate what we ought to listen to. And there are, sadly, many Christians who are willing to abdicate their thinking privileges to others, too lazy to decide for themselves.

I believe it is every Christian's right and responsibility to decide how he or she will live in the world. This is part of the freedom Christ came to give us. It should not be abandoned or abused.

When it comes to music, we should all be aware of what we are listening to and how it is affecting us. For those not used to paying such close attention to what is being heard, it will mean making a conscious effort to discern a song's message as well as its emotional effect. This can be done by simply asking a few questions:

> What am I feeling?
> Is this healthy?
> Is this consistent with my faith?
> Does this song's message go against any of the basic truths Christians live by?

A conscious effort to answer those questions should result in the ability to judge whether or not to continue listening to a particular song or a certain group.

Deciding that a song has a true message does not mean merely that we agree with what is being said or that it makes us feel good. A song may have a true message yet makes us uncomfortable. For example, knowing that millions of the world's people are starving is not particularly pleasant to think about, and does not make anyone feel good. It is true nonetheless — as demonstrated by the song 'Do They Know It's Christmas?' the Geldof/Ure Band Aid anthem. On the other hand, a Christian song implying that 'if you'll only trust Jesus he'll give you everything you want,' might invoke good feelings, even though it offers a false message. A song is not true just because it has the words *Jesus* or *God* in it. Neither is a song false because it omits those words.

As I have said before, each song must be examined carefully to determine the message.

Once a song is found to be unacceptable, must it be censored? The answer to that question is, maybe. Only the individual listener can determine that, and each must decide for him or herself, depending on his or her own inner strength. For example, if a song is very persuasive, and you find yourself doubting something you know to be right, then you may act as your own board of censors and cut it out of your programme. However, another Christian may find the song unobjectionable; he or she may not be affected in the same way as you are. You cannot decide that another Christian should not listen to it; you can only decide for yourself and explain, if asked, why you think the song is harmful.

If we wish to be allowed the freedom to listen (or not to listen) to the music we choose, then we must allow others to make their own choices, too. We must do this not only for the sake of tolerance and respect for the freedom of others, but because it is foolish to set ourselves up as the supreme arbiter of such matters. Instead, we should let God be the final authority.

Many have been vocal in condemning rock music. They have written books; they have preached sermons; they have spread the word far and wide: Rock is no good. It is too weird, too wanton, too wrongheaded to be used by God. It's anti-Christian, and therefore irredeemable for Christian use.

In spite of the fact that this book has been devoted to presenting a reasoned approach to the subject of how rock music can play a significant role in the lives of Christians, the reason I am absolutely convinced that the critics are wrong in their use of shock horror scare stories to condemn all rock music is because of my own personal experience.

After all, I have been touched by Christian rock music; it spoke to me at a time in my life when nothing else did. In a real sense it changed my life. For although I was a Christian, there were huge areas of my life where God was not in control. Then one night I heard a Christian rock group playing in a park. I sat down and listened, and a new person went home that night. I was moved toward a deeper relationship with God, and I have always considered that night, and that group with their music, a turning point. They showed me that it was possible to live as a Christian in the modern world without being irrelevant, old-fashioned or hopelessly bound by unquestioned dogma.

Since then I have attended many concerts where I have seen others touched in the same way I was; I have seen people built up through rock music. I have received letters from people whose lives have been healed by God speaking through Christian rock music and rock musicians. I have seen God's hand moving among thousands of people in this way. I have seen contemporary Christian music incorporated into church worship. I have seen Christian musicians become a presence and a force for good in the rock music industry.

How can one lightly find fault with the methods God so repeatedly uses to reveal himself?

The Bible tells the story of a visit Jesus made to the home of his good friends, Mary, Martha and Lazarus. Jesus was greeted by Martha and welcomed into their home. She scurried around looking after all the preparations for the big meal she had planned. I suppose that as she hurried to get things in order, it suddenly dawned on her that she was working alone — where was Mary? She looked up and there was Mary sitting with Jesus, deep in conversation with him. Martha was immediately angry; she was doing her part, and here was Mary, chatting idly away with so much yet to be done. 'Lord, doesn't it seem unfair to you that I have to do all the work while Mary just sits?' she asked. And before Jesus could even respond, she answered the question herself, saying, 'Tell her to come and work with me.'

Although Mary and Martha were sisters, with a common background, heritage and family life, they were different people. Although they both loved Jesus and were loved by him, they expressed that love in different ways: Martha through serving Christ's physical needs, and Mary in communion with him. And I think Jesus appreciated them both, one just as much as the other. He did not expect them to act the same or to love him in the same way: he knew they were different. He knew there was a place for Martha in the kitchen, and a place for Mary in the parlour. But there was no place for one to sit in judgment over the other. That is why Jesus said, 'Martha, dear friend, you are upset over all these details. There is really only one thing worth being concerned about. Mary has discovered it, and I won't take it away from her.' Loving him was the important thing, and he was not about to discourage Mary, or make her join her sister in the kitchen.

We must allow others to serve Christ and express their love for him in ways that are natural to them, and therefore best for them. It is not fair to expect all believers to express their faith and their love for Christ in the same way. It is equally unfair to judge other Christians because their expressions of love and faith are different from our own. Martha's sin was not so much in worrying over details but in condemning Mary for not doing as she did. Jesus offered her a gentle reprimand and declined to choose sides in the matter. He understood that for faith to be meaningful, people had to be able to honour and worship God freely in their own way.

We must arrive at this same tolerance regarding music. Our musical tastes are our own. No Christian should be belittled for liking rock; conversely, those who like rock should refrain from condemning music which others find meaningful.

If we are to love as Christ loves, then we must accept those with differing musical tastes and accept their right to listen to the music they mind meaningful. Rather than condemning rock, God's people should be in the position of encouraging whatever is good, worthy and true in popular music. Where wrongs have been committed, where error is practised, we need a vigorous demonstration of the truth. Rather than blacklisting, condemning, or otherwise shackling our Christian artists, we must encourage them to higher achievement. For the Christian community and the world at large desperately need the creativity, enthusiasm, courage and vision Christian artists can bring.

Notes

Chapter 3

[1] Jonathan Eisen, *The Age of Rock* (New York: Random House, Vintage Books, 1969), p. 126.
[2] Tony Palmer, *All You Need Is Love: The Story of Popular Music* (New York: Penguin, 1976), p. 217.
[3] Ibid.
[4] 'G-Man Blues: Elvis Wanted to Help,' *Time*, 24 July 1978, p. 23.

Chapter 4

[1] Bob Larson, *The Day Music Died* (Carol Stream, Ill.: Creation House, 1972), pp. 87-88.
[2] Palmer, *All You Need Is Love*, p. 7.
[3] Ibid., pp. 5-6.
[4] Bruno Nettl, *Music in Primitive Culture* (Cambridge, Mass.: Harvard University Press, 1956), p. 128.
[5] Kate Hevener, 'The Affective Character of Major and Minor Modes in Music,' *American Journal of Psychology* 47 (1935), pp. 103-118.
[6] Larson, *The Day Music Died*, p. 111.
[7] William S. Kroger and William D. Fezel, *Hypnosis and Behavior Modification* (Philadelphia: J. B. Lippincott, 1976), p. 291.

Chapter 5

[1] Ian Whitcomb, *After the Ball* (New York: Simon and Schuster, 1972), p. 202.
[2] John Rublowsky, *Popular Music* (New York: Basic Books, 1971), p. 95.
[3] Whitcomb, *After the Ball*, p. 202.
[4] Jane Stuart Smith and Betty Carlson, *A Gift of Music* (Westchester, Ill.: Good News Publishers, 1978), p. 128.

Chapter 7

[1] J. G. Machen, *Christianity and Culture* (Huemoz, Switzerland: L'Abri Fellowship, 1969), p. 4.

Chapter 8

[1] Richard Stanislaw, 'Should We Rock the Boat over Rock Music?' *Eternity*, March 1977, p. 25.

Chapter 9

[1] Paul Johnson quoted by Thomas Spurr in 'Gospel Music: Alive and Well,' *Charisma*, July-August 1978, p. 46.

[2] M. Goldbeck in Erik Routley, *Twentieth Century Church Music* (New York: Oxford University Press, 1964), p. 114.

[3] Charles Etherington, *Protestant Worship Music* (New York: Holt, Rinehart and Winston, 1962), pp. 3-4.

[4] Cyril Barnes, *God's Army* (Elgin, Ill.: David C. Cook, 1978), p. 100.

Chapter 10

[1] Francis Schaeffer, *Art and the Bible* (London, Hodder and Stoughton, 1973).

Frameworks for living series

'Direct access to live issues'

David Porter
USER'S GUIDE TO THE MEDIA
How to enjoy and evaluate soaps, adverts, news, the message.
- Don't scrub soap
- What a friend we have in Volkswagon
- I photograph best from the left
- More is said than what is spoken

Joyce Huggett
LIFE IN A SEX-MAD SOCIETY
Handling intimacy, sex and friendship.
- The petting problem
- Cooling the sex urge
- Is sexual sin unforgivable?
- The pain of splitting up

J. John
DEAD SURE? about yourself, life, faith.
A credible explanation of Christianity for today.
- Modern problems
- Anxiety, stress, loneliness
- The Jesus story in modern English
- No resurrection – No Christianity
- Why believe?

Alan MacDonald with Tony Campolo,
Val Howard and others
THE TIME OF YOUR LIFE
- Getting more from pop and film
- Enjoying sport and friends
- Social times and social action
- The place of drink and parties